Autumn Rites

Volume I

Celtic Worlds

Karol Kolbusz

Cover art: *A Walk at Dusk* by Caspar David Friedrich.

TABLE OF CONTENTS

ACKNOWLEDGMENTS

The author would like to express his heartfelt gratitude to Ryan Dziadowiec for proofreading the entire text and suggesting additions and modifications.

INTRODUCTION

It is beyond a shadow of a doubt that the modern world is a place full of misery, suffering, and hopelessness. We are living in an atomised, rootless, and directionless society, in which nothing is valued more than frenetic money-making and shallow, carnal pleasures. Millions of people are suffering from depression, anxiety, and countless deep-seated psychological traumas.

What is the primary reason for the growing epidemic of meaninglessness and nihilism, then? It is modern man's disconnection from his own spiritual and cultural roots. The traditional teachings of ancient Greek, Roman, and Vedic philosophers and sages no longer capture his dispersed attention. The citizen of the digital century is deeply averse to spiritual authority. He is lost and sinking in the quicksands of modernity and unrestricted technological progress, which is inversely proportional to his happiness. Yet, in his arrogance, he refuses to listen to those who could potentially show him the right way. Similarly, the myths and folk tales of ancient Celtic and Germanic origin, immensely rich in meaning, depth, and beauty, are being shunned in favour of the newest blockbusters and electronic gadgets. The modern man has not just forgotten his roots, but he has also strayed away from the path of *dharma*.

Dharma can be understood as a cosmic law, with neither beginning nor end, which permeates and applies to all animate beings and inanimate objects in the universe. It is a supra-individual, metaphysical order that sets the physical world in a state of balance and harmony, protecting it from forces of chaos and dissolution. The concept of *dharma* stands in direct opposition to the current materialistic paradigm in science, according to which the universe is a mechanism devoid of any inherent meaning and purpose. The consequence of the latter worldview is ethical relativism and rejection of the notion that metaphysical principles and laws form the basis of reality. From such a limited point of view, we are born as mere pieces of flesh and bones that are left clueless and helpless in the face of the vast universe. *Dharma*, on the other hand, is a holistic natural law based on the premise that the universe is an extremely intelligent design rooted in transcendence. Many of the ancient civilisations, and particularly those of Indo-European origin, were *dharmic* in nature – meaning that all aspects of social life (religion, politics, science, law, literature, war, agriculture, etc.) within them were constructed in consonance with *dharma*. Due to obvious racial, cultural, and linguistic differences, this universal law manifested itself in a slightly divergent way in each civilisation. There was a time on Earth, however, when people across Europe and Asia were ruled by virtuous kings whose reign was strengthened by this primordial, sacred law.

In order to empower people with meaning, hope, and strength, and to contribute to the restoration of forgotten *dharmic* principles, I have decided to write a tetralogy of haiku poetry inspired by Indo-European cultural and spiritual heritage. The present volume focuses on ancient and early medieval Celts.

Haiku is a traditional Japanese three-line poem form with seventeen syllables, written in a 5/7/5 syllable count. Often focusing on natural images, haiku stresses clarity, intensity, and directness of expression.

The purpose of this work is following:

1) To put the readers in a contemplative mood, which will hopefully encourage them to appreciate the beauty of nature, do more to protect the environment (lest we are deprived of its sanative power), and to slow down, despite the omnipresent obsession with speed and action. As the title of this book, *Autumnal Rites*, suggests, the poems are related to the themes of transition, departures, harvest, solitude, mystery, and ageing. Haiku poems, with their meaningful simplicity, are an excellent tool that can potentially help us lead a more meditative and satisfactory life.

2) To acquaint the readers with the pre-Christian cultural heritage of ancient and early medieval Celts. In this volume, I have also chosen to write about Celtic Christianity, for this — predominantly monastic — religious tradition is inextricably intertwined with the cultural framework of early medieval Britain and Ireland. Each haiku (with the exception of miscellaneous poems) is followed by a commentary section, which aims to explicate the meaning and significance of a given tradition, custom, historical event or a deity. The additional explanations are meant to encourage and inspire the reader to research these topics in greater depth and detail. At the end of the book, I include a list of suggested further reading.

3) To encourage the readers to understand and appreciate the darker side of life, which often comes onto the surface during autumn. Typical autumnal atmosphere of incessant rain, bone-chilling wind, and dense fog facilitates our transition from the familiar warmth and solar brilliance of summer days into the odd and the unknown of fall. The terseness of haiku poetry and its emphasis on surprise, contrast, and epiphany can greatly

stimulate our imagination and enhance our sensitivity to psychic phenomena. Poems in this volume were inspired by a multitude of cultural works, including the tales of mystery and macabre by H. P. Lovecraft and Edgar Allan Poe, as well as the surreal films of David Lynch. Moreover, a large amount of inspiration has been derived from the musical works of Alan Stivell, a well-known Breton harpist, and the electronic music of Richard D. James (Aphex Twin) and Mike Paradinas (μ-Ziq).

4) To acquaint the readers with the richness and diversity of Celtic languages, as well as dialectal and provincial forms of British English. In addition to that, many archaic and rare words are referenced and explained throughout the book. Their choice is meant to enhance the experience of venturing into the past centuries.

5) To stress the crucial importance of spiritual practice and devotion to the deities in the ancient world, as well as to show how, according to the ancients, the metaphysical affected the physical. The textual and archaeological evidence from Classical Antiquity demonstrates that gods were far from being distant and indifferent, and they actively participated in the world. They were not just archetypes, symbols, and role models, but also real metaphysical beings, aspects and manifestations of the pure and formless God. Haiku poems, with their focus on describing beautiful, yet meaningful, transitory moments can perfectly illustrate how the eternal influences the temporal.

In my opinion, the ultimate solution to the crisis of modernity is the restoration of *dharma* on all levels – which includes, quite literally, bringing the gods of our ancestors back. Naturally, this process should not be done mechanically and thoughtlessly. We must consider the reality of the modern world. That being the case, the nature of pre-Abrahamic, *dharmic* deities is perennial – they have always existed and will continue to exist, so long as the world turns. They wait to be re-discovered, for metaphysical reality is neither contingent nor subject to change.

Autumnal Rites is the second part of a seasonal tetralogy. Due to the lack of space to contain all the poems I wrote, I have decided to split *Autumnal Rites* into four separate volumes, each dedicated to one particular culture. It is my hope that those who seek beauty, knowledge, and inspiration will find *Celtic Worlds* and its sequels interesting and thought-provoking.

PART ONE

GAUL

Mercurius Moccus

Acorns and beechnuts
on the sunlit forest floor;
ominous shrill squeals

Commentary

In ancient Gallo-Roman religion, Moccus was the divine protector of boars and pigs, as well as boar hunters. Often identified with the Roman deity Mercury, he might have been the tribal god of the Lingones, a Gaulish tribe which dwelt around the rivers Seine and Marne in present-day north-eastern France. In ancient Gaul, the boar was a widely revered animal— it was a popular symbol on battle standards, *carnyces* (long horns), coins, and helmets. The ferocity and strength of this animal may suggest a metaphorical connection with warfare.[1] According to the French metaphysician René Guénon, however, the wild boar symbolized the representatives of spiritual authority among the ancient Celts.[2]

The haiku poem above depicts a seemingly peaceful woodland glade somewhere in the tribal territory of the Lingones. Oaks and beeches grow plentifully there, and they have recently dropped their respective acorns and beechnuts. Yet the serene atmosphere is disrupted by a herd of wild boars, signalling their approach to the glade. Acorns and beechnuts have a high carbohydrate content, which is essential for the build-up of body fat reserves needed to survive the winter. Boars gorge on these nuts as well as earthworms and insects, using their powerful snout and tusk to dig into the earth. Wild boars are primarily nocturnal and crepuscular, meaning that they prefer to forage either at night (their peak activity is around midnight) or at dusk and dawn. During the day, they rest in burrows or hollow shelters which they make in stands of tall grass or leaf litter.

---

1   M. Green, *Symbol & Image in Celtic Religious Art* (London: Routledge, 1989), p. 139.

2   R. Guénon, *Symbols of Sacred Science* (Hillsdale, NY: Sophia Perennis, 2004).

Ogmios

The bard's heartfelt song
rouses the hall's listless folk;
bleak deluge outdoors

Commentary

In the religion of the ancient Celts, Ogmios was the deity of speech, eloquence, and persuasion. He may have been the divine patron of bards. Ogmios is often described as the Celtic counterpart of the Greeks' Hermes and the Romans' Mercury. The satirical writer Lucian drew a comparison between Ogmios and Heracles, the latter being the Greek half-god and hero. He described Ogmios as resembling an older, more tanned version of Heracles. This Celtic mythological figure also had long chains running from his tongue to the ears of his followers. This is clearly a Mercurial attribute, denoting the deity's magnetic power of persuasion and binding. Despite these differences, both Ogmios and Heracles wear lion skins and carry a bow and club in their hands. According to some scholars, Ogmios' role extended to that of a *psychopomp*, the one who escorts the newly deceased from the terrestrial life to the otherworld.

The setting of the poem is a Gaulish *oppidum* (a fortified settlement), located somewhere in Auvergne, the land of the Arverni. They were one of the most powerful Gaulish tribes. In 52 BCE, the Arvernian chieftain Vercingetorix spearheaded the unsuccessful insurrection against Julius Caesar and the impending doom of Roman supremacy over Gaul. Having forged alliances and exchanged hostages with many Gaulish tribes, Vercingetorix assumed the command of the uprising and led the united Gaulish army against the Romans. After an initial victory at the Battle of Gergovia, Vercingetorix was defeated by the Romans at the battle of Alesia. As a result of the revolt's failure, the Arverni lost their formal independence and the entirety of Gaul was subdued, becoming a Roman province shortly after.

The poem, set some months before Vercingetorix's uprising, depicts an eloquent Arvernian bard who reminds his compatriots about the glorious deeds of their ancestors. The pouring November rain, incessantly blasting upon the roof of the chieftain's hall, parallels the worsening *esprit de corps* of the Gaulish population. Being a devotee of Ogmios, the god of speech and persuasion, the bard skilfully manages to revive the morale and ancestral pride among the Arvernians.

Mercurius Artaius

Chilly mountain stream —
sharp claws tear the trout apart
while wild ducks depart

Commentary

In ancient Gallo-Roman religion, Artaius was a deity of regional prominence, whose name suggests association with bears.[3] He is known from a single inscription from Beaucroissant in south-eastern France, where he is syncretised with Mercury. The scant evidence suggests that Artaius might have been the divine patron of bears and hunting.

The setting of the poem is a cold stream in an autumnal setting, somewhere in the French Alps. The brown bear successfully manages to catch the unwary trout and consumes it afterwards. The migration of the wild ducks is a *kigo*, meaning a phrase that is associated with a particular season. It is widely utilised in traditional forms of Japanese poetry in order to indicate the season referred to in the stanza.

During late summer and autumn, brown bears actively build up fat reserves needed to survive winter. Although they are omnivorous animals, they rely mostly on non-animal sources of food. Their diet includes berries, acorns, grasses, pine cones, mushrooms, roots, and bulbs. When it comes to animal matter, brown bears consume insects, larvae, bugs, beetles, ants, honey bees, wasps, and moths. Large prey items consist of salmon and trout, small rodents, hares, ground-nesting birds, deer, and boars. The fishing techniques of browns bears are well-studied. They often lurk around falls when the fish are forced to breach the water, at which point the bears will try to catch the fish in mid-air. They will also wade into shallow waters, attempting to clasp a slippery fish with their claws.

---

3   From Gaulish artos, meaning "bear". The name Artaius itself means "ursine".

Carnutes

Long thunderous horns
disperse the cloud of dense mist
that shrouds their white robes

Commentary

The Carnutes (meaning "the horned ones") were a significant Gaulish tribe, whose territory was located between the Sequana and Liger rivers. Their name possibly derives from Gaulish *carnon* ("horn"). Carnotium (or Autricum), an important Carnutian *oppidum* (a fortified settlement), is the present-day city of Chartres, known for its impressive medieval cathedral. Cenabum, another principal stronghold of the Carnutes, had been sacked and razed by Julius Caesar in 52 BCE. It was then rebuilt by emperor Aurelian in 273-274 CE. The town's new name — *civitas Aurelianorum* — later evolved into Orléans.

According to Julius Caesar's report, Gaulish druids met annually in a sacred location in the land of the Carnutes, in the middle of Gaul.[4] It is said that every Gaul who had a dispute came to this place from every region, and submitted to the druids' decisions and judgments. The druids were traditionally depicted as white-cloaked religious leaders, though their societal role extended to that of historians, judges, astronomers, and teachers. Caesar also mentions that all druids were ruled by a chief druid who had supreme authority among them.

The haiku poem above describes the annual druidical procession taking place near the town of Carnotium. Early morning mist (which symbolises the air of secrecy and obscurity surrounding these esoteric druidical rites) is metaphorically dispersed by the loud sound of the long horns. The latter are *carnyces* (sing. *carnyx*) — large trumpets, usually made of bronze and

---

4   J. Caesar, *The Gallic War*, 6.13.

brass and shaped like the head of an animal. They were widely utilised in the Iron Age Celtic world, mainly for military and ritual purposes. Due to the thunderous and harsh sounds they made, *carnyces* were used to raise the army's morale and to intimidate enemies.

The poem was inspired by Alan Stivell's song *Druidic Lands* (from the artist's album *Explore*).

Cicolluis

Beams of dazzling light
slant on the giant's broad chest;
tranquil evening falls

Commentary

In ancient Gallo-Roman religion, Cicolluis was a martial deity associated with qualities such as strength and protection. His name means "great-breasted". In the *interpretatio romana*, Cicolluis was syncretised with Mars. The haiku poem above describes a colossal statue of Cicolluis towering above a sleepy Gaulish village. The depiction was inspired by Pliny the Elder's report of a gigantic bronze statue of Mercury erected in Gaul by the Greek sculptor Zenodorus. According to Pliny:

"[…] All the gigantic statues of this class have been beaten in our period by Zenodorus with the Hermes or Mercury which he made in the community of the Arverni in Gaul; it took him ten years and the sum paid for its making was 40,000,000 sesterces. Having given sufficient proof of his artistic skill in Gaul he was summoned to Rome by Nero, and there made the colossal statue, 106 feet high, intended to represent that emperor but now, dedicated to the sun after the condemnation of that emperor's crimes, it is an object of awe".[5]

---

5   Pliny, *Natural History*, 34. 45.

Apollo Atepomarus

She soaks her rough hands
in the crystalline hot spring;
a soft, muffled neigh

Commentary

In ancient Gaulish religion, Atepomarus was a god associated with healing and horses. His name means "Great Horseman" or "possessing a great horse". In the Roman period, he was syncretised with Apollo. At some healing sanctuaries, small figurines of horses were given to him as votive offerings. Atepomarus is mentioned in numerous inscriptions from Gaul. He might have been the tribal god of the Bituriges (meaning "kings of the world" or "kings of blacksmithing"), who inhabited the central part of Gaul.

The haiku poem above depicts an elderly woman seeking relief from rheumatoid arthritis. She visits a holy spring dedicated to Apollo Atepomarus. Having given a small figurine of a horse in offering to the deity, she proceeds to soak her swollen hands in the hot spring. Miraculously, the horse-god's acceptance of the oblation manifests in the quiet sound of neighing nearby.

Rudianos

The blood-stained stallion
charging blindly at the foes
all trembling with fear

Commentary

In ancient Gaulish religion, Rudianos was a deity worshipped in south-eastern France. The name *Rudianos* means "red", reflecting the martial nature of the deity. A prehistoric image of a mounted war-god, perhaps Rudianos himself, was found at Saint-Michel-de-Valbonne. The finding was dated to the 6th century BCE. The menhir-shaped stone depicts a roughly carved figure of a rider with a large head, riding down five severed heads. According to classical writers, ancient Celts hung the severed heads of their defeated foes from their saddles.

Aerecura

Horn filled with ripe fruit
slung round the maiden's torso;
evening homecoming

Commentary

In the religion of the ancient Celts, Aerecura (or Erecura) was a chthonic goddess of fertility and abundance. She is often depicted with attributes of fertility such as the *cornucopia* (horn of plenty) and baskets filled with apples. Aerecura is usually depicted in a seated posture, wearing a full robe and bearing trays or baskets with ripe fruit. Her chthonic attributes make her similar to Hecate and Proserpina, other goddesses of the underworld. Most attestations of Aerecura are found in the Danubian area of Southern Germany and Slovenia, though they also occur in Italy, Great Britain, and France. Dedications to her are concentrated around Stuttgart and along the Rhine. Furthermore, several monuments in honour of Aerecura occur in cemeteries or other funereal contexts.

The haiku poem above depicts the personification of Aerecura — a young Celtic woman from southern Noricum (present-day Slovenia) is coming home with ripe fruit gathered in the nearby orchard.

Nantosuelta

Windings of the stream
in the montane beech forest;
croaks pierce the cool air

Commentary

In the religion of the ancient Celts, Nantosuelta was a goddess venerated primarily in Gaul. She is often shown in the company of Sucellus, the Gaulish mallet-wielding god. Some scholars have demonstrated a parallel with the Irish divine couple, the Dagda and Morrígan, who shared similar attributes with Sucellus and Nantosuelta. In art, Nantosuelta is depicted with a raven and holding a round house on a pole. The round house may have symbolized abundance. Other representations show her with a pot or beehive. It is thought that Nantosuelta, much like her Irish counterpart Morrígan, transformed into a crow on the battlefield. Additionally, the Gaulish goddess is frequently associated with water and portrayed as being surrounded by water. Her name is usually translated as "of the winding stream".

The haiku poem above depicts a chilly stream that snakes through a beech forest, located somewhere in the lower parts of the French Alps. The cawing of crows circling above the woods indicates that Nantosuelta is the divine protectress of this area.

Ritona's Blessing

A windless forenoon —
cows have crossed the placid ford
where old willows grow

Ritona's Bane

Mooing at the ford —
thorn stuck in the calf's pastern
all red and swollen

Commentary

In the religion of the ancient Celts, Ritona was a goddess worshipped mainly in the lower valley of the Moselle river, in the land of the Treveri tribe. A temple dedicated to her was excavated in the Roman city of *Augusta Treverorum*, present-day Trier. At Crain, in north-central France, archaeologists have found a funeral stela of a man making an offering to Minerva and Ritona. The etymology of her name suggests that she might have been a divine protectress of fords and water crossings.

The haiku poems above, set in Gaul during the 2nd century BCE, depict a tranquil ford on a small brook. The first poem shows the benefic aspect of Ritona — a herd protected by the goddess successfully manages to cross the ford. In the second poem, however, an injured calf is mooing for its mother's attention. The locals have neglected the worship of Ritona and now the goddess exhibits her malefic aspect.

Icovellauna

Twinkling golden coin
rolling down the spiral stairs;
soft mirroring splash

Commentary

In ancient Gaulish religion, Icovellauna was a goddess worshipped mainly in the valley of the Moselle river of eastern Gaul. An octagonal temple at Le Sablon in Metz, originally built over a spring (which has long since dried up), was dedicated to her. A spiral staircase led down to the water level, allowing devotees to deposit votive offerings and draw from the sacred spring. One of the statuettes discovered at the base of the temple was that of a local deity interpreted as Mercury. It is not known what the name of this deity was or whether he was considered a consort of Icovellauna. However, the association of Mercury with healing strongly suggests that Icovellauna was a goddess of healing waters. In addition to that, the name Icovellauna is often translated as "Divine Source of the Waters".

The haiku poem above is set during a sunny September afternoon sometime in the Roman period. A visitor to the shrine of Icovellauna accidentally drops a golden coin. The *aureus*[6] rolls down the spiral staircase and eventually lands in the sacred spring. A brief flash of reflected sunlight is seen as the twinkling coin softly hits the water.

---

6   *Aureus* was a gold coin and monetary unit used in ancient Rome. It was regularly issued from the 1st century BCE to the beginning of the 4th century CE.

Ucuetis

A rainy twilight —
flames of the blacksmith's forge
fanned by montane wind

Commentary

In ancient Gaulish religion, Ucuetis was a deity associated with craftsmen and blacksmiths. He was worshipped at Alesia in Burgundy and his female consort was the goddess Bergusia. An epigraphic dedication to the couple, carved on a bronze vase, was found in the cellar of a large hall. Rubbish discovered in this underground room was made up of bits of bronze and iron and seems to have been part of the metalsmiths' stock. It has been suggested that the cellar was a shrine to the local crafts-deities of Alesia, and the great building itself may have been a guild hall of blacksmiths and other artisans.

The haiku poem above depicts a rainy November twilight in the blacksmith's forge at Alesia. The poem was partially inspired by Skyforge, an ancient forge in the town of Whiterun, which can be found in the video game *The Elder Scrolls V: Skyrim*.

Ankou

The black-robed coachman
halts his rain-soaked draught wraiths
by the hangman's house

Commentary

In Breton folklore, the Ankou is a spectral being who is the henchman of Death. In each Breton parish, the spirit of the last dead person of the year becomes the Ankou of his or her community for the duration of the following year. The Ankou is usually portrayed as a tall, haggard creature in a white hat with long white hair. It is either male or female. Sometimes the spectre is depicted as a skeleton with a revolving head. There are many tales involving the Ankou, though in most versions it drives a creaking cart piled high with corpses. The wagon, pulled by four black horses, stops at the house of someone who is about to die, so that the Ankou can collect that person's soul. The 19th-century writer Anatole le Braz suggested that the Ankou is a survival of the prehistoric dolmen-builders of Brittany.

The haiku poem above depicts an inclement November dusk in an isolated hamlet in Brittany. The Ankou drives up to a house where a downtrodden young man is about to hang himself.

Azénor

Golden-haired princess
locked in the umbral tower;
hushed prayers and tears

White dress stirred by breeze
reveals her bare, dainty feet;
ascending the stake

The sobbing crowd gasps —
in vain the servants breathe out
to emblaze the stake

Into the unknown —
a boat without oars and sails
floats through the high sea

An aureate coast —
waves splash over her fair locks
as she lies senseless

Commentary

The noble Even, lord of Brest in Brittany, had only one child, named Azénor. Around 537 CE, she married the Count of Goëlo. The newly-wed couple set themselves up in a large castle. After being widowed, Even remarried, and Azénor's stepmother never ceased to embarrass her stepdaughter. Jealous, she swore to get rid of Azénor. She accused her of infidelity with the help of false witnesses. The count of Goëlo believed this defamation and the princess was locked up in the keep's darkest tower. She was condemned to death by burning at stake. However, servants present at the execution were unable to kindle the stake; it was deemed bewitched by Azénor.

When it was learnt that the princess was pregnant, the judges were probably bribed into sentencing her to be put into a barrel and set adrift at sea. The barrel floated for five months. Each day, Saint Brigid visited Azénor to bring her all she needed. After a dangerous voyage, Azénor landed on the bank of the Beauport in Ireland, where she delivered a son. She named him Budoc, meaning "saved from the waters". On her deathbed, Azénor's stepmother revealed the truth to the Count of Goëlo. In consequence, he decided to set out to look for Azénor in order to pardon her. However, he died on their return after having long sought for her. Even welcomed his grandson Budoc to his court and raised him to nobility. Later in his life, Budoc became a great saint.

The haiku poems above were inspired by Alan Stivell's song *Azénor* (from the artist's album *Legend*).

Mont-Saint-Michel

Treble of the bells —
waves hitting against the rocks
veiled by rosy haze

A peaceful noontide —
sheep graze on the salt marshes
dappled in soft warmth

Tenor of the bells —
an old monk gazes blankly
at the bedimmed sun

Commentary

Mont-Saint-Michel is a rocky tidal island and famous abbey located off the coast of Normandy. Although it is often said that an Irish Christian hermit founded the original site, its actual history is more ancient. A few kilometres north of Mont-Saint-Michel lies another, smaller island called Tombelaine. According to one possible etymological explanation, the toponym Tombelaine could derive from *tumulus belenis*, meaning "the tomb of Belenos", Belenos being a widely-worshipped Celtic deity. The most popular translation of the deity's name is the "bright or shining one", derived from a Proto-Indo-European root *bhel* "to shine", interpreting Belenus as a deity solar in origin.

Interestingly enough, Belerion was the name used by ancient Greek and Roman writers to describe the south-western tip of Britain. Menez-Dol, a prominent granite massif located near Mont-Saint-Michel, was identified with *Mons Iovis*, mentioned by the 9th-century Welsh monk Nennius. According to scholars, *Mons Iovis* was a peak consecrated to Taranis, a Celtic god of thunder, who is often equated with the Roman Jupiter. Given the available evidence, it is plausible to attribute religious importance predating the Christian era to this area.

Prior to the erection of the first monastic establishment in the 8th century, Mont-Saint-Michel was an Armorican stronghold of Gallo-Roman culture. However, the Franks ravaged it, thus ending the trans-channel culture that had flourished since the departure of the Romans in 460 CE. From approximately the 5th to the 8th century, Mont Saint-Michel belonged to the territory of Neustria. A medieval legend states that the archangel Michael appeared in 708 to Aubert of Avranches, the bishop of Avranches, and commanded him to establish a church on the tidal rock. In the early 9th century, it was a place of political significance in the marches of Neustria.

Mont-Saint-Michel gained strategic significance again in 933 when William I Longsword, the Duke of Normandy, annexed the Cotentin Peninsula from the weakened Duchy of Brittany. The isle is depicted in the famous Bayeux Tapestry, which commemorates the Norman conquest of England. Harold Godwinson is shown on the tapestry rescuing two Norman knights from the quicksand in the tidal marshes during a battle with Conan II, Duke of Brittany. The patronage of Norman dukes funded the abbey's magnificent architecture in subsequent centuries. The abbey of Mont-Saint-Michel became both a major pilgrimage site (souvenirs have been sold here since the Middle Ages) and a locus of ecclesiastical and political power. It was also an influential centre of medieval education, with a rich library and scriptorium. During the Hundred Years' War, the church developed into a military citadel. As an impregnable fortress in the sea, it was the only spot in Normandy that never surrendered to the English.

The three poems above depict Mont-Saint-Michel at dawn, noon, and dusk, respectively. They were inspired by Aphex Twin's track *Mt Saint Michel + Saint Michaels Mount* (from the artist's album *Drukqs*).

Sheep in the second poem are *agneau de pré-salé* (French: "Salt meadow lamb"), a kind of lamb raised in salt meadows below Mont Saint-Michel. The pastures are covered in halophyte grasses with a high salinity and iodine content, causing the lamb to have a distinct taste that is considered a delicacy.

PART TWO

CORNWALL

The Tin Route I: Belerion

Bal at the tall cleeves —
leatherwings fly noiselessly
in the growing dusk

Commentary

Belerion was the name used by ancient Greek and Roman writers to describe the south-west tip of Britain. It is not known whether the term referred to Land's End or the region of Cornwall in its entirety. According to the Sicilian Greek historian Diodorus Siculus (c. 90 BCE – c. 30 BCE), who was probably quoting Pytheas of Massalia (4th century BCE), the land of Belerion was famous for its tin mining and dealings with foreign merchants. Indeed, Cornwall and neighbouring Devon had vast reserves of tin, which was extracted extensively during the Bronze Age by people associated with the Beaker culture. Tin is required to make bronze from copper, and by about 1600 BCE the West Country was undergoing a trade growth driven by the export of tin across Europe. Tin mining continued in the region through the Iron Age, the time of Roman domination in Britain, and later centuries, until it ended with the closure of South Crofty mine in 1998.

The haiku poem above depicts a former Cornish mine (*bal* in the Cornish dialect) at Botallack, perched at the top of tall cliffs (*cleeves* in the Cornish dialect). As the night falls, bats (*leatherwings* in the Cornish dialect) emerge out of the mine's ruined engine houses.

This poem was inspired by Alan Stivell's song *The Tin Route* (from the artist's album *Beyond Words*).

The Tin Route II: Ictis

At the beach market —
the swarthy merchants inspect
glowing tin ingots

Commentary

Ictis or Iktin was an island off the coast of south-west Britain described by Diodorus Siculus as a tin trading centre. After the tin was extracted in the aforementioned land of Belerion, the charcoal-burners smelted the ore into astragal-shaped ingots. The ingots were then transported to the beach market at Ictis. Modern scholars continue to debate the island's location. Several possible candidates have been suggested: St Michael's Mount and Looe Island off the coast of Cornwall, the Mount Batten peninsula in Devon, and the Isle of Wight further to the east.[7]

The haiku poem above depicts Phoenician merchants examining tin ingots at the beach market at Ictis. Even though occasional Mediterranean sailors might have travelled to Britain (Pytheas of Massalia was one of them), it is important to remember that the trade of the Phoenicians and Greeks with the island was indirect. They relied on Venetian brokers from Armorica (Brittany) who transported ingots across the English Channel and then over land through Gaul. According to Julius Caesar:

"These Veneti exercise by far the most extensive authority over all the sea-coast in those districts, for they have numerous ships, in which it is their custom to sail to Britain, and they excel the rest in the theory and practice of navigation. As the sea is very boisterous, and open, with but a few harbours here and there which they hold themselves, they have as tributaries almost all those whose custom is to sail that sea."[8]

---

7   M. Aldhouse-Green, *The Celtic World* (London: Routledge, 1995), p. 276

8   J. Caesar, *The Gallic War*, 3.8.

Merlin's Cave

As high tide recedes
coruscating rays clear out
the zawn's pitch darkness

Commentary

Merlin's Cave is situated beneath Tintagel Castle in Cornwall. It is a sea cave sculpted by marine erosion along a thrust plane between slate and volcanic rocks. Though the grotto is flooded with water at high tide, it has a sandy floor and is reachable at low tide. It goes all the way through the rock, and there is a smaller cave off it that can be entered from the southern side. Alfred Tennyson immortalised Merlin's Cave in his *Idylls of the King*, depicting waves bringing the infant Arthur to the shore and Merlin carrying the future king to safety in the castle above.

In the Cornish dialect, a *zawn* is a fissure or cave in a coastal cliff. The haiku poem describes how, during one warm September afternoon, brilliant rays of the sun pierce through Merlin's Cave, illuminating its pitch-black interior.

I would like to thank my friend Amy Dyer for providing me with inspiration for this poem.

St Materiana's Church

Strings of pale sunlight
colour the austere chancel;
crashing of the waves

Commentary

The haiku poem above depicts St Materiana's Church, a Norman temple perching high atop the cliffs overlooking the village of Tintagel. The remoteness of the site, an open landscape, the proximity of sea waves crashing upon the cliffs, and the large graveyard south of the building make the church one of the most spectacular sights of Cornwall.

A Roman milestone bearing the name of Emperor Licinius (who died in 324 CE) was found at the site. Originally, the landmark was built into the church lychgate where it had been used as a coffin rest. It was discovered in 1889 and moved inside the church for preservation. The first church may have been a 6th-century oratory founded by monks from the nearby Minster. A Saxon stone church replaced it afterwards, and the site was used as a Christian graveyard over the next centuries. The present building dates to the late 11th century, though its design includes some earlier Saxon features. In the Norman period, St Materiana's church was simply a chancel and nave with a small north-east chapel added soon after. In the 14th century, transepts were added, giving the church a cruciform shape.

The poem describes the weak autumnal sun filtering through the chancel's stained-glass windows. The rays give the otherwise austere interior a mellow look.

The Merry Maidens

Indistinct crooning —
icy breeze pats lone longstones
sprinkled with starlight

Commentary

The Merry Maidens is a late neolithic or early Bronze Age stone circle located near the village of St Buryan in Cornwall. The circle, which is regarded to be complete, consists of nineteen granite megaliths. They are aligned three to four metres apart with a larger gap between the stones on the east side. The circle is roughly twenty-four metres in diameter. To the south is another stone which may indicate a possible north-south orientation.

A local legend explains the origin of the stones; nineteen maidens were transformed into stone as punishment for dancing on a Sunday. In the Cornish dialect, *merry maiden* is another word for a mermaid or siren. The Pipers, two menhirs in the proximity of the Merry Maidens, are thought to be the petrified remains of the musicians who played for the dancers. According to another tale, the two stones were erected following a 10th-century battle in which the Anglo-Saxons, led by Æthelstan, fought the Cornish Celts, led by Howel and supported by the Danes. The Pipers were said to signify the positions of the two opposing leaders.

The setting of the haiku poem above is a frosty, starry night, sometime in November. Legend has it that on such nights the stones appear to make sounds that resemble quiet singing or humming. In the Cornish dialect, the word *longstone* refers to a standing stone or a menhir. The poem was inspired by Aphex Twin's track called *Merry Maidens*.

Spriggan

Abandoned tin mine —
a sharp hiss fills the crisp air
as the sky murkens

Commentary

In Cornish folklore, the *Spriggans* were malicious spirits depicted as deformed, wizened old men with big child-like heads. They were thought to have their dwellings in ancient ruins, abandoned tin mines, cairns, and barrows where they guarded buried treasures. Despite their relatively unimpressive physical appearance, they were reckoned to be the spirits of giants and retained enormous strength. Sometimes they exhibited the ability to grow to immense size.

Spriggans were notorious for their unpleasant characters. They enjoyed causing mischief against those who offended them. They raised sudden whirlwinds to horrify travellers, created storms to destroy crops, and sometimes kidnapped human children, leaving their ugly changelings in their place. They were blamed if a house was burgled or a building collapsed, or if cattle were stolen.

A modern depiction of these creatures can be found in the video game *The Elder Scrolls V: Skyrim*, in which the *Spriggans* inhabit large forested caves and pits.

The haiku poem above depicts a solitary *Spriggan* dwelling in an abandoned tin mine in Cornwall.

Morgawr

The fish jowster's eyes
widen in feeble rushlight;
low growl on the quay

Commentary

In Cornish folklore, Morgawr is a sea serpent that allegedly inhabits the sea near Falmouth Bay in Cornwall. The origin of the legend can be traced to 1876, when an unnamed fisherman from Falmouth maintained that he caught a huge sea creature. In more recent times, the beast was said to have appeared near Pendennis Point in 1975. It was depicted as having a trunk with a very long neck and black or brown skin. Local mackerel fishermen blamed adverse weather conditions and poor fishing on supposed sightings of the monster. According to other versions of the story, the Morgawr appeared after German submarine U28 torpedoed a British merchant ship during World War I. The most recent sighting of the Morgawr was in 1999. A man known as John Holmes, a former Natural History Museum worker, claimed he videotaped an unidentified sea creature.

In the Cornish dialect, the word *jowster* means "itinerant seller". The haiku poem above, set in medieval Cornwall, depicts how the itinerant fish merchant witnesses the appearance of a mysterious aquatic creature, a historical antecedent to the Morgawr.

The Owlman

A touch of light frost —
a hellish screeching echoes
through the grim churchyard

Commentary

A remote church in the village of Mawnan in Cornwall is rumoured to be the dwelling place of an owl-like creature which has been frightening locals and tourists since 1976.

The legend originated in 1976 when two teenage girls, on holidays with their parents in Mawnan Smith, walked down to the old and remote church, more than a mile from the village centre. On the top of the church tower, they saw what was described as a terrifying "bird-man", with wings and feathers. The girls were so frightened by the sighting that their father decided to put an end to their holidays and leave Cornwall immediately. Occasional claims of Owlman sightings in the vicinity of the church circulated in 1978, 1979, 1989, and 1995. According to one story, a "loud, owl-like sound" could be heard at night in the nearby Mullion churchyard in 2000.

The haiku poem above depicts the piercing cry of a Eurasian eagle-owl hovering above the church tower at Mawnan one November midnight. The owls prefer to nest in older churches, where they can find safe shelter in the architectural nooks and crannies. These animals favour rural areas with arable land and pastures, which are optimal feeding grounds. Conversely, they tend to avoid locations with high light pollution and have busy road networks nearby.

Allantide

While skeat dims the goons
the scent of steamed apples
fills the crowded pub

Commentary

Allantide (Cornish: *Nos Kalan Gwav*, meaning "eve of the first day of winter"), also known as Saint Allan's Day or the Feast of Saint Allan, is a Cornish festival that was traditionally observed on the night of October 31. Allantide is the liturgical feast day of St Allan (also spelt St Allen or St Arlan), who was the bishop of Quimper in the 6th century. The festival is most likely the Cornish equivalent of the Gaelic feast of *Samhainn*.

Prior to the celebration, Allan Markets were held in some Cornish towns and villages. These markets frequently sold large, highly polished red apples called Allan apples. Some people would purchase an Allan apple and wait until Allantide to eat it. Others would gift them to their families and friends, believing they might bring good luck. Allan apples could also have romantic significance. Older girls would place them under their pillows, hoping to dream of the person whom they would one day marry. Other children thought that if they didn't sleep with an Allan apple under their pillow on Allantide, they might experience bad luck.

Some sources record a local game, in which two pieces of wood were fastened together in the shape of a cross. They were then suspended with four candles on each outcrop of the cross shape. Afterwards, Allan apples were hung under the wooden cross. Those who participated in the game were to catch the apples in their mouth, with hot wax being the penalty for slowness or inaccuracy.

Many divinatory practices are associated with Allantide. It was customary during that time to throw walnuts into the fire to predict the fidelity of partners. Another tradition involved pouring molten lead into cold water and interpreting the shape of the solidified lead to learn the occupation of future husbands.

The haiku poem above, set during Allantide, depicts a remote pub near the fishing town of St Ives in Western Cornwall. In the Cornish dialect, the word *skeat* means "a heavy fall of rain", while *goon* refers to a flat downland or an unenclosed pasture, usually shared between farms. In the poem, people gather in the local pub to shelter from the autumnal downpour that made the moorland look bleak and desolate. Some of them may also want to taste the steamed Allan apples, prepared by the pub owner's wife.

The Beast of Bodmin

The rising full moon
shines on the mossy longstone;
a shadow creeps past

Commentary

In modern Cornish folklore, the Beast of Bodmin was a feline creature purported to live on Bodmin Moor and the surrounding area. Alleged sightings of the Beast of Bodmin and occasional reports of mauled livestock began around 1978. Dozens of sheep and calves had been killed in a peculiar way, which could not have been attributed to dogs. The creature was rumoured to be a large black cat resembling a panther or a puma. It had sharp, prominent teeth and yellow eyes. A government-funded investigation was carried out in 1995. As a result, no verifiable evidence for the presence of exotic felines in Britain was found. Furthermore, the investigators suggested that the mutilated farm animals could have been attacked by common indigenous species.

The haiku poem above depicts the Beast of Bodmin spotted within King Arthur's Hall, which is a megalithic enclosure located on Bodmin Moor, near the civil parish and village of St Breward. The moorland itself is dotted with numerous prehistoric cairns, barrows, and stone circles. King Arthur's Hall measures twenty meters wide and forty-seven meters long. Fifty-six out of a possible one hundred and forty of the vertical stones are still visible today. They resemble the backs of chairs – hence the name of the monument, which alludes to the legendary Round Table – and face inwards from a steep-sided rectangular bank. Many of the stones have collapsed and still more may have been concealed due to the bank slumping. King Arthur's Hall is thought to be a late Neolithic or early Bronze Age site.

In the Cornish dialect, the word *longstone* refers to a standing stone or a menhir.

Exmoor Nights

A twittering shrew
dashes to the yeavy nook;
the kestrel's swift dive

Commentary

Exmoor is a vast area of hilly moorland in north-western Somerset and northern Devon. Exmoor was designated a National Park in 1954. It borders the Bristol Channel on the north and has a picturesque coastline of rugged hills interspersed with narrow, wooded valleys. Inland, beyond the fringe of farms, lies a hazy plateau of heather uplands, rising more than 300 metres above sea level. The moors are utilised as pastures for hardy Exmoor ponies and Exmoor horned sheep. The wide array of wildlife on Exmoor includes buzzards, kestrels, barn owls, herons, red deer foxes, hares, otters, and shrews. Moreover, Exmoor National Park is an excellent location for astronomical observations, owing to its status as an International Dark Sky Reserve. On cloudless nights, a visitor to Exmoor can see myriads of stars and other celestial objects.

The haiku poem above depicts a small shrew (a small mammal resembling a mouse) fleeing from the kestrel hunting it. In the dialects of Cornwall and Devonshire, the word *yeavy* means "damp" or "watery".

Saint Nectan's Glen II

Dry leaves in the stream;
ethereal murmurings
of the twilit falls

Commentary

Saint Nectan was a 5th-century south-western Brythonic hermit, traditionally associated with a secluded woodland glen (near Tintagel in Cornwall), which was named after him. It is believed that he had his hermitage above the waterfall, the glen's most spectacular and picturesque feature of natural interest. Moss and ferns grow on the rocks surrounding the waterfall. According to hagiographic sources, Nectan owned a small silver bell which he kept in a high tower. He would ring it during stormy weather in order to warn ships that would otherwise have been smashed on the rocks at the mouth of the Rocky Valley. Yearning for solitude, the early medieval Irish and Brythonic hermits often sought out remote and serene places of pristine beauty.

The haiku poem above depicts Saint Nectan's Glen in autumn. Fallen leaves partially obstruct the flow of the stream above the waterfall, altering the sound of water cascading into the pool. The atmosphere of the poem was inspired by Aphex Twin's track *14 cornish spreek5b [St. Nectan's Glen Waterfalls mix]*. Additional inspiration was derived from μ-Ziq's track *Ethereal Murmuring*s.

In late 2019, I wrote another haiku depicting Saint Nectan's Glen. The poem is included in my book *Wintertide Rites*.

PART THREE

WALES

Silures

The black-haired chieftain
slays the scared eagle-bearer;
wild cries in the storm

Commentary

The Silures were a powerful tribal confederation of ancient Wales. They occupied south-east Wales and perhaps some adjoining areas. They were neighboured to the north by the Ordovices, to the east by the Dobunni, across the Bristol Channel to the south by the Dumnonii, and to the west by the Demetae.

The Silures actively resisted the Roman conquest from about 48 CE. A Roman legionary fortress was established first at Glevum (Gloucester) and later at Isca (Caerleon), in the middle of their tribal territories. Despite that, the Silures continued to wage effective guerrilla warfare against the Romans. Sextus Julius Frontinus eventually subjugated them in a series of campaigns ending about 78 CE. According to Tacitus, however, the Silures *were changed neither by cruelty nor by clemency*. Tacitus has also reported that the Silures had a swarthy complexion and curly hair.[9] Due to their distinct appearance, the Roman writer believed that they had migrated from Spain at an earlier date.

The haiku poem above depicts a fierce battle between the Romans and the Silures, in which the Silurian leader kills the Roman eagle-bearer. An *aquilifer* was a soldier carrying the eagle standard of a Roman legion. The name derives from the type of insignia, *aquila* meaning "eagle", and *fers*, related to the Latin word for bringing or carrying. The eagle standard was the most important possession of the legion, and its loss was regarded as the ultimate shame and disgrace.

---

9   Tacitus, *Agricola*, 11.

Caer Wydyr

Grim fortress of glass —
silent sentries guard the walls
swathed in cool twilight

Commentary

In Welsh mythology, Caer Wydyr (or Caer Siddi) is the name of a legendary Otherworld fortress mentioned in Middle Welsh poems in the *Book of Taliesin*. It was said to be a castle made of glass, whose battlements were swarming with silent, uncommunicative watchmen (possibly representing the risen dead). Caer Wydyr was completely dark except for one dim light given off by the lamp burning before its circling gate. Some scholars have attempted to give the fortress a physical location, for example as the island of Grassholm off the coast of Pembrokeshire in Wales, or even as Glastonbury Tor in England. It is, however, more likely that Caer Wydyr is a poetic depiction of the Celtic Otherworld.

Déisi

Sharp darts pierce his heart
as he hides coins near the cliffs;
bronze horns harshly blare

Commentary

An Irish tale, *The Expulsion of the Dessi*, gives an account of the migration of the tribe, usually known as the Déisi, from southern Ireland to Dyfed in southwestern Wales under Eochaid mac Artchorp. Traditionally, the establishment of the Irish dynasty in Dyfed was dated to about 270 CE. The recent tendency, however, has been to place the migration of the Déisi at the very end of the fourth or beginning of the 5th century, when the Roman rule in Britain was coming to an end. The Irish, who had long been harassing the Welsh coasts, found that there was no longer any formal opposition to them, so they moved into the vacuum.[10]

In the late 3rd century, hoards of coins were buried for safe-keeping along the western coasts of Wales. They were never recovered by their owners who had presumably been slain or taken into slavery by the Irish.[11] The haiku poem above, set in the early 4th century, depicts an Irish raiding party about to sack a Brythonic settlement on the southwestern Welsh coast. A local homesteader attempts to bury his valuables in the soil near the cliffs. He is, however, killed by the raiders, and his treasure is quickly found. In ancient and medieval Ireland, darts (*ga*) were widely utilised in warfare.

---

10   L. Alcock, *Arthur's Britain* (Harmondsworth: Penguin Books, 1987), p. 123.

11   *Ibid.*, p. 93.

Castell Henllys

The bard's mournful tale —
the sound of crwth by the hearth
far from pelting rain

Commentary

Castell Henllys is an Iron Age inland promontory fort in northern Pembrokeshire, Wales.

The *crwth* is a type of traditional Welsh instrument. It is a bowed lyre about the size of a violin. Though originally plucked, it was played with a bow from the 11th century, and a fingerboard was added behind the strings in the last part of the 13th century.

The haiku poem above depicts a gloomy November evening in Castell Henllys, sometime in the early medieval period.

Ceffyl Dŵr

Hoof prints in the mud —
lashing rain in the churchyard
swamped with dawn's dullness

It is almost dark —
chill rises from the damp soil
in hallowed stillness

Screeching of the owl —
white horse amid cold tombstones
buried in deep fog

Commentary

In Welsh folklore, the *Ceffyl Dŵr* is a mythical water horse, a counterpart of the Scottish *kelpie*. It is thought that the creature inhabits mountain pools and waterfalls. Even though it appears solid, it can quickly evaporate into mist. According to some accounts, the *Ceffyl Dŵr* leaps out of the water to trample and kill unwary travellers. The perception of the creature varies — in North Wales, it is considered dangerous and malevolent, whereas the folk of South Wales see it in a more positive light.[12]

The setting of the poems above is St Illtyd's Church, located near Oxwich, a village in the county of Swansea in South Wales. Although it is said that a 6th-century Celtic monastic cell originally stood on this site, the first written reference to the church dates back to the 10th century. The sheep-tending Cistercian monks rebuilt the temple in the late 12th century,

---

12   M. Trevelyan, *Folk-lore and Folk-stories of Wales* (Wakefield, EP Publishing, 1973).

and most of what one can see today dates back to this period. In the churchyard, a dried-up well is rumoured to be haunted. A ghostly white horse was said to appear in the churchyard and then vanish mysteriously in the well.

The haiku triad above depicts the appearance of the *Ceffyl Dŵr* in the churchyard. The poems intend to convey an atmosphere of gloominess and mystery felt by a visitor to the church in late November.

Dinas Emrys

Cascading rainbow —
two newts hidden in vapour
merged with pale sunlight

Lush hills in russet —
a short-tailed blindworm basking
on the mossy rocks

Commentary

The rugged hillfort of Dinas Emrys is located on one of the principal routes through Snowdonia in northern Wales. Archaeological excavations unveiled several stone walls and revetted terraces surrounding a small summit. The stone foundations of an oval structure were discovered on the peak, as well as a square pool or cistern, several post-holes which were probably part of a palisade, and other structures whose dating and function remain uncertain. The dating of objects found on the site ranges from the early Roman to the medieval periods. The former consist of pottery, glass, an iron brooch, and three rein rings from a chariot. Late Roman and early medieval finds include gilt-bronze studs, mortars, Romano-British pottery, at least seven glass containers, and a two-handled amphora.[13]

According to legend, when Vortigern fled into Wales to escape the Anglo-Saxon invaders, he chose this high place as the site for his royal fastness. Every evening the royal masons would lay down their tools only to return the next day to find they had vanished and their carefully erected walls had collapsed. Day after day, the problem persisted. Eventually, Vortigern was recommended to seek the help of a young boy not conceived by a mortal man. A search was launched across the land, and the boy they

---

13   C. A. Snyder, *An Age of Tyrants* (Stroud: Sutton Publishing, 1998), p. 188-189.

found was called Myrddin (Merlin). Vortigern was advised to sacrifice the boy in order to appease supernatural powers that prevented him from building a fortress here. Myrddin, however, convinced the king that the hillfort could not stand due to a hidden pool containing two dragons. The beasts were said to be engaged in perpetual battle, destroying the foundations of the stronghold in the process. The boy explained how the White Dragon of the Saxons — though winning the battle at present — would soon be killed by the Welsh Red Dragon. After Vortigern's death, the fort was given to High-King Ambrosius Aurelianus, known in Welsh as *Emrys Wledig*, hence the name of the hillfort.

Another local tale has it that Myrddin hid treasure in a cave at Dinas Emrys. The discoverer of the treasure will be "golden-haired and blue-eyed". When that specific person is near Dinas Emrys, a bell will toll to invite him or her into the cave, which will open of its own accord.

The first haiku poem above depicts a real-life pool, which is located beneath Dinas Emrys. A dramatic and picturesque waterfall cascades into the pool, and the poem describes how, after the pouring rain, the pale sun comes out and forms a small rainbow. Miraculously, two smooth newts (*Lissotriton vulgaris*) emerge out of the evaporating haze. Newts are amphibians, reproducing in ponds and puddles during the spring. They spend the rest of the year feeding on invertebrates in wooded areas, hedgerows, and damp meadows. Newts are frequently seen on damp days or after a rain. These animals hibernate underground (often in congregations of several newts) among tree roots and in old walls.

The second haiku poem above depicts the ruins of Dinas Emrys, set against the autumnal background of wooded hills. A blindworm (*Anguis fragilis*) is basking on the mossy remains of the stone wall. Blindworms are usually active during twilight, though they occasionally bask in the sun when weather permits. However, they are more often found hiding beneath rocks and logs. These carnivorous lizards feed on worms and slugs. The "blind" in blindworm refers to the animal's tiny eyes. A blindworm's skin is smooth with scales that do not overlap one another. Like many other lizards, they autotomize, meaning that they can shed their tails to evade predators. Even though the tail regrows, it does not reach its original length.

Lake Glaslyn

Sparks of dazzling light
in the pellucid blue tarn;
low clouds veil the cirque

Commentary

Glaslyn is a glacial lake located in Snowdonia, North Wales. It is the source of Afon Glaslyn, the major river of Gwynedd. In Welsh folklore, Arthur had Bedivere throw his magical sword Excalibur into Glaslyn, where Arthur's body was later put in a boat to be carried away to Avalon. Then, Arthur's men retreated to a cave on the slopes of Y Lliwedd (rising above Glaslyn), where they are said to sleep until they are needed.

Sparks of dazzling light in the first line of the poem do not refer to the sunshine (since low clouds obscure the lake), but rather to the glimmering light of Excalibur, held by the Lady of the Lake.

The haiku poem above was inspired by Alan Stivell's song *La dame du lac* (from the artist's album *The Mist of Avalon*).

The Death of Maelgwn Gwynedd

Vile yellow-eyed *gwyll*
crawls through the dismal marshes;
strange breath of foul wind

The boarded-up church —
flickering candle goes out
as cool breeze comes up

Banging at the door —
signs of utter fear consume
the king's frenzied eyes

Though the sun is up
a deathly silence prevails;
murk swallows all life

The door bursts open —
lances of blazing sunlight
cut the foetid corpse

Commentary

Maelgwn Gwynedd was an early 6th-century king of Gwynedd, a Brythonic kingdom in north-west Wales. His name means "Princely Hound". After the dissolution of Roman authority in Britain, North Wales was left defenceless against the incursions of Gaelic raiders from Ireland. According to tradition, the origins of the kingdom of Gwynedd can be traced to Maelgwn's great-grandfather Cunedda Wledig. Around 400 CE, Cunedda and his sons are said to have migrated to Wales from *Manau Guotodin* (present-day Clackmannanshire in Scotland). They brought a substantial degree of stability to Brythonic rule in northern Wales, though it was not until the late 5th century that the Irish were fully expelled.

What we know about the reign of Maelgwn Gwynedd is mostly derived from *De Excidio et Conquestu Britanniae* ("On the Ruin and Conquest of Britain"), a work written in Latin by the 6th-century British cleric St Gildas. In his scathing critique of post-Roman rulers, Gildas writes that Maelgwn left his first wife and throne to become a monk. However, he broke his monastic vows and returned to the secular world with violence. Maelgwn overthrew and slew his paternal uncle, the king, and married the uncle's widow. Furthermore, Gildas scorns Maelgwn for revelling in praise of his sycophantic court poets and neglecting the Church. In reality, however, Maelgwn was a generous supporter of Christianity, financially supporting the foundation of many churches throughout Wales and even far beyond the borders of his kingdom.

According to a legend, Maelgwn died of the Yellow Plague in 547 CE. Fearing for his life, he retreated to a small church in Llan Rhos and shut all the windows and doors. One night, he heard a strange banging at the door. When he looked out through a hole, he saw a *gwyll*, a terrifying yellow-eyed beast which personified the Yellow Plague, and fell into a long sleep. His attendants waited for days. When they realised his silence had been too long for sleep, they broke into the church and found the king's rotting corpse.

The haiku poems above retell the story of Maelgwn's death, depicting how the yellow-eyed monster arrives from the nearby salt marshes to bring death to the king. The poems were inspired by David Lynch's *Mulholland Drive*. In the infamous diner scene, a man tells another about a nightmare in which he dreamt of encountering a horrific figure behind the diner. When they investigate whether the dream had any grounding in reality, the monster comes out from behind the restaurant, causing the man who had the nightmare to collapse in fright.

Din Orwig

Pounding fills the hills —
the blacksmith swings his hammer
in the brisk dawn air

Commentary

Din Orwig (or Dinorwic) is a small village located in Snowdonia, North Wales. The settlement is famous for the nearby slate quarry, which is the second-largest quarry of this kind in Wales. The extraction of slate in this area had already begun in the Roman era when it was used for the construction of the Segontium fort. The first modern attempts to mine here started in 1787 and at its peak, Din Orwig slate quarry employed over 3000 men. A massive surge in demand for slate roofing tiles in the late 19th century meant tiles were exported all over the UK, Europe, and even North America. The quarry closed in July 1969 as a result of industry decline and the growing difficulty of slate removal.

The name of the hamlet means "Fort of the Ordovices". The Ordovices were an ancient Celtic tribe that inhabited northern and central Wales by the time of Roman invasion. They were partially subdued by the Roman governor Gnaeus Julius Agricola in the campaign of 77-78 CE. The name of the tribe is connected with the word "hammer", possibly referring to their skill of making hammers or mining. Alternatively, it may indicate that the Ordovices fought with sledge-hammers.

The haiku poem above depicts an early October morning in modern Din Orwig. An elderly village blacksmith is working in his workshop, unconsciously tapping into the ancestral craft of his ancient Celtic forebears.

Hiraeth

The flight of wild geese —
wistful knights at the bleak court
in the windswept hills

Commentary

Hiraeth is a Welsh word referring to a feeling of nostalgia, wistfulness, and homesickness. It also describes a yearning for home that one cannot return to, no longer exists, or maybe never was.

The haiku poem above, set sometime in the middle of the 12th century, depicts a remote Welsh court (*llys*) belonging to a local prince (*tywysog*). His armed retainers (*teulu*) stand beside the tall, earthen ramparts. Gazing eastwards, they point wistfully to *Lloegyr*, the part of England that belonged to their ancestors many centuries ago. The departing wild geese heighten the wistful atmosphere of this bleak October day. Remembering their ancestral deeds and yearning to reclaim *Lloegyr*, they experience *hiraeth*.

In contrast to most countries in Europe at the time, the style and tactics of medieval Welsh warfare was only marginally influenced by feudalism. Welsh military terminology reflected the cultural continuum of earlier, pre-Roman traditions and early medieval Celtic culture persisting into the High Middle Ages. Moreover, it would have been challenging for heavily-armoured feudal knights to travel and wage war effectively in the mountainous territory of Wales.

The Welsh forces which faced Anglo-Norman incursions were based around the individual chieftains' armed retainers (*teulu*). The rest of the army would consist of any able-bodied local men over the age of fourteen. Military service was seen as a privilege, as opposed to feudal militias who perceived it as an obligation.

Ysbryd

Rest in the drab keep —
as the embers cease to glow
white ghost haunts the walls

Commentary

The haiku poem above depicts Dolbadarn Castle, a large fortification built by the Welsh prince Llywelyn the Great during the early 13th century. The castle was erected at the base of the Llanberis Pass, overlooking the lake of Llyn Padarn in northern Wales. Traditionally, the Welsh monarchs had not built stone fortifications. However, from the late 11th century onwards the growing danger of Norman conquest necessitated their construction. Welsh castle-builders relied on the conveniently rugged terrain of the Welsh countryside as their principal means of defence. Therefore, Welsh strongholds were situated in remote spots, frequently roosted high on rocky outcrops, protected by cliffs, and defended by deep-cut ditches.

In 1284 Dolbadarn was captured by Edward I, who removed some of its timbers to construct his new castle at Caernarfon. The castle was utilised as a manor house for some years, before falling into ruin. In the 18th and 19th centuries it was a popular destination for painters.

In the Welsh language, the noun *ysbryd* means "spirit", "ghost". The poem above is set sometime in the 18th century. A travelling painter decides to sleep in the dilapidated keep of Dolbadarn Castle. As soon as his campfire dies out, a ghost appears on the ruined walls.

Blodeuwedd

Cold, enormous eyes —
sharp rays of the sinking sun
pierce the dark owl hole

Commentary

In Welsh mythology, Blodeuwedd (also Blodeuedd) is one of the central characters in the Middle Welsh wonder tale, *Math fab Mathonwy*, the last of the *Four Branches of the Mabinogi*. She was a beautiful girl created from flowers as a wife for Lleu Llaw Gyffes. Lleu's mother had put a curse (*tynged*) on him that he may never have a human wife. Blodeuwedd was created to counteract the curse. She was unfaithful, however, and conspired with her lover Gronw Pebr to murder Lleu. The attempt failed, and Blodeuwedd was turned into an owl as a punishment.

The setting of the haiku poem above is a tranquil dusk-tide on a small farm (*pentre*) in Mid Wales. The hole in the poem is an architectural feature that allows owls access into farm buildings such as barns or mills. The ultimate purpose of this design is to provide nest sites for barn owls (*Tyto alba*) so that they can prey on farm vermin. Owl holes, first used at the end of the 17th century, were frequently situated on the gable ends of buildings. The perch or landing platform was constructed from stone or wood and usually sloped slightly downward to prevent rain from entering the building. The entry holes permitted owls to enter with space for a safe landing and passage to the interior. At the same time, their specific size excluded the intrusion of undesirable predators. Nowadays, few owl holes are still in active use. Due to the advent of pest control chemicals, the perceived value of biological pest control has drastically decreased.

Caer Arianrhod

Moon shows the steep path
to the bemisted stronghold
spiraling skywards

Commentary

In Welsh mythology, Caer Arianrhod is the legendary abode of
Arianrhod, a lunar goddess and heroine portrayed in early Welsh literature.
It was said to be a spiral tower on the sea, and folk belief has it that it was
located off the coast of Gwynedd in North Wales. Those who enter Caer
Arianrhod find it very difficult to leave of their own volition. Those who
manage to return, however, bring with them the gift of prophesy. Taliesin
claims to have visited this magical castle three times to gain the arts of
clairvoyance and poetry. In Welsh, Caer Arianrhod is also a popular name
for the constellation Corona Borealis.

Castell Dinas Brân

Flowers in her plaits
ruffled by warm western wind;
loud sound of hoof beats

The knight-errant's horse
leads through the sylvan hillside
flecked with sun's last rays

Loose strands of fair hair
fall on the knight's white palfrey;
the crow's cry at dusk

Her lustrous blue eyes
avert the knight's steely gaze;
tears stain the kirtle

Commentary

Castell Dinas Brân is a medieval castle situated on a rugged hilltop site above the town of Llangollen in Denbighshire, Wales. Dinas Brân has been variously translated as the "crow's fortress" or "fortress of Brân", with Brân being the name of a deity or a nearby stream. Welsh castle-builders relied on the conveniently rugged terrain of the Welsh countryside as their principal means of defence. Therefore, Welsh strongholds were situated in remote spots, frequently roosted high on rocky outcrops, protected by cliffs, and defended by deep-cut ditches.

A large hillfort was built on the hill around 600 BCE during the Celtic Iron Age. An earthen rampart, probably with a wooden palisade, surrounded several roundhouses. An extra-deep ditch was cut to protect the gentler slopes on the southern side of the hill. Despite the lack of archaeological evidence, it has been suggested that in post-Roman Britain, the hillfort was the residence of Elisedd ap Gwylog, an 8th-century king of Powys. In the 13th century, the early fortifications had largely been replaced by a medieval castle, probably built by Gruffudd ap Madog, ruler of north Powys. In 1277 the castle was besieged and destroyed by Henry de Lacy, Earl of Lincoln. The Welsh defenders burned the castle so that the English would not be able to use it and retreated before de Lacy's troops arrived. The castle was not severely damaged by the fire, however. It was abandoned after 1282 when the castle of Holt on the Dee was built as the centre of a new lordship. It was never repaired and quickly fell into ruin.

The haiku poems above depict an imaginary romance tale taking place in Castell Dinas Brân. A fair-haired princess stands at the battlements of the fortress. Yearning for the homecoming of her beloved knight, she looks wistfully westwards. When the chivalrous man eventually arrives at the keep, the princess notices that something about his eyes has changed. They are cold and steely. Intuitively sensing some illicit affair, she bursts into tears. A palfrey is a type of horse that was highly valued as a riding horse in the Middle Ages. It was a lighter-weight horse, suitable for long-distance travel.

The poems were inspired by Aragorn's arrival at Edoras in J.R.R. Tolkien's *Lord of the Rings*, as well as Peter Jackson's cinematic illustration of this scene.

Dyrnwyn, the Sword of Rhydderch Hael

Crisp October night —
the white hilt bursts into flames
making the thief scream

Commentary

Dyrnwyn, the Sword of Rhydderch Hael, was one of the *Thirteen Treasures of the Island of Britain*, a set of magical items in late medieval Welsh tradition. It was an enchanted blade belonging to Rhydderch Hael, a 6th-century ruler of Alt Clut, which was an early medieval kingdom in southern Scotland. When drawn, the blade burst into flames; if drawn by a noble man, the fire would help him in his cause, but its fire would burn the man who drew it for a mischievous purpose.

The haiku poem above depicts a thief who, unaware of the blade's magical properties, attempts to steal Dyrnwyn.

The Hamper of Gwyddno Garanhir

The grand feast goes on
though the garreted servant
fails to shut the gates

Commentary

The Hamper of Gwyddno Garanhir was one of the *Thirteen Treasures of the Island of Britain*, a set of magical items in late medieval Welsh tradition. If a person was to put food for one man in the basket and open it again, it would contain food for one hundred men.

According to tradition, Gwyddno Garanhir was the lord of Cantref Gwaelod, a legendary kingdom located off the west coast of Wales. His chief fortress was known as Caer Wyddno, somewhere to the north-west of modern-day Aberystwyth. The whole kingdom was protected from the sea by floodgates, which had to be shut before high tide. One day the keeper of the floodgates, Seithenyn, was drunk and failed to close them, with the result that the sea swept in and flooded the land.

The haiku poem above depicts the adverse consequences of using the magical basket. The multiplication of food prolongs the feast at Caer Wyddno, causing the gate-keeper to get drunk. Intoxicated, he forgets to shut the floodgates before high tide, and consequently Gwyddno's kingdom is flooded. The archaic adjective *garreted* means "slow-witted".

The Horn of Brân Galed

The bewildered sot
gazes at the centaur's horn
filled with heady wine

Commentary

The Horn of Brân Galed was one of the *Thirteen Treasures of the Island of Britain*, a set of magical items in late medieval Welsh tradition. The horn was said to have possessed the magical quality of ensuring that whatever drink might be wished for was found in it. Legend has it that Hercules had extracted the horn from the head of the centaur he had slain, whose wife then killed the Greek hero in bloody revenge. According to Welsh tradition, Myrddin had approached the kings and lords of Britain to request their treasures. They agreed on the condition that he obtained the legendary horn of Brân Galed, assuming that the task would be impossible to fulfil. However, Myrddin somehow succeeded in acquiring the drinking horn and so received the other treasures as well. He took these artefacts to the Glass House (*Tŷ Gwydr*), where they would remain forever. Myrddin's Glass House is traditionally believed to be Bardsey Island, which is located three kilometres off the Llŷn peninsula in north Wales.

The haiku poem above depicts a filthy drunkard who, driven by his insatiable lust for intoxication, manages to break into the Glass House.

The Chariot of Morgan Mwynfawr

Before the dawn's light
rumbling of the chariot
fades in the grey hills

Commentary

The Chariot of Morgan Mwynfawr was one of the *Thirteen Treasures of the Island of Britain*, a set of magical items in late medieval Welsh tradition. The chariot is described as a magical vehicle which would swiftly reach whatever destination one might desire to go to. Morgan ab Athrwys, also known as Morgan Mwynfawr ("Morgan the Generous"), was an 8th century king of Morgannwg in south-east Wales.

The Knife of Llawfrodedd Farchog

Fresh blood at the feast —
twenty-four nobles butchered
with knife plunged in pork

Commentary

The Knife of Llawfrodedd Farchog was one of the *Thirteen Treasures of the Island of Britain*, a set of magical items in late medieval Welsh tradition. Llawfrodedd Farchog was a hero of Welsh tradition and a legendary figure in Arthur's court. His knife was able to simultaneously serve twenty-four men at the dinner table. The meaning of the personal name *Llawfrodedd* is not known, though it has been suggested that it is a misspelling of *Llawfrydedd*, meaning "sorrow". The hero's epithet *Farchog* can either mean "horseman" or "bearded".

The haiku poem above demonstrates that the legendary utensil could also have been used for more sinister purposes. In the poem, twenty-four nobles invited to Llawfrodedd's feast are magically butchered with the knife.

The Coat of Padarn Beisrudd

Ambush in the woods —
a Pict's arrow whizzes past
the purple-robed king

Commentary

The Coat of Padarn Beisrudd was one of the *Thirteen Treasures of the Island of Britain*, a set of magical items in late medieval Welsh tradition. According to one interpretation, *Padarn Beisrudd ap Tegid* (meaning "Paternus of the Scarlet Robe, son of Tegid") may have been a Celtic chieftain who was granted Roman military rank, a practice attested elsewhere along the empire's borders at the time. Padarn is believed to have been born around 400 CE in northern Britain. Tradition has it that the Coat of Padarn Beisrudd perfectly fits any brave and noble man, while it does not fit on cowards and ruffians. An additional property is that the coat protects the wearer from harm.

The haiku poem above depicts a group of Pictish brigands attempting to kill Padarn Beisrudd in an ambush. However, the latter is protected by the magical coat and manages to evade the ambush.

The Chessboard of Gwenddoleu ap Ceidio

The eve of slaughter —
ornate pawns play the chess game
in an empty room

Commentary

The Chessboard of Gwenddoleu ap Ceidio was one of the *Thirteen Treasures of the Island of Britain*, a set of magical items in late medieval Welsh tradition. The board was made of gold, while the pieces were made of silver and crystal. It is said that the pawns may play by themselves if they are set up correctly. Gwenddoleu, son of Ceidio, was a 6th-century Brythonic king of a small kingdom located near present-day Carwinley, north of Carlisle in Cumbria. In 573 CE, Gwenddoleu was killed in the disastrous battle of Arfderydd. Overwhelmed by grief, his bard Myrddin Wyllt ("Merlin the Wild") went mad and fled into the Caledonian Forest, where he lived as a hermit. Myrddin is sometimes identified with Merlin the Wizard from Arthurian legends.

The haiku poem above depicts how Gwenddoleu's pawns play the chess game that mimics and foreshadows the disaster at Arfderydd.

PART FOUR

SOUTHERN BRITAIN

Tamesis

Sparkles of sunlight
dive into the Thames' deep bed
where a bronze shield rests

Commentary

The Thames, the second-longest river in the United Kingdom, was known in Roman times as *Tamesis*. Throughout history and prehistory, the Thames has been an important river, both as a route for travel and commerce. The significant number of Late Bronze Age swords found in the river implies that by 1000 BCE it had become a centre for a widespread Celtic rite of watery oblations. A substantial number of Iron Age finds have been extracted from the Thames, such as the Battersea and Wandsworth shields and the Waterloo Bridge helmet, as well as many examples of high-quality swords and other metal objects. The fact that so many luxury items, most likely associated with a social elite, were deposited in the river shows that it probably had some religious meaning. Moreover, the Thames was an important entry point into Britain, with many imported products first appearing around the Thames estuary. It may also have served as an easily-defended natural boundary, and presumably formed the southern border of the Catuvellauni and the Trinovantes tribes.[14]

The haiku poem depicts the aforementioned Battersea shield deposited at the bed of the river. The shield was dredged from the bed of the Thames in London in 1857. A large number of Roman and Celtic weapons and skeletons was found in the same location. At the time, it was thought that the area was the site of Julius Caesar's crossing of the Thames during the 54 BCE invasion of Britain. Nowadays, however, it is believed that the shield was a votive offering which probably predates the invasion.

---

14   J. Koch, *Celtic Culture. A Historical Encyclopedia* (Santa Barbara and Oxford: ABC-CLIO, 2006), p. 1667.

Tridamos

The three-horned auroch comes into the radiance of golden ploughed fields

Commentary

In ancient Romano-British religion, Tridamos was a deity associated with fertility and supposed bovine triplication (three-horned cattle). In etymological terms, the name of the deity is derived from the Proto-Celtic *Tri-damos*, meaning "threefold bovine one". It has been suggested that Tridamos may have been a Brythonic equivalent of Tarvos Trigaranus, which was a Gaulish deity portrayed either as a three-horned bull or a bull surrounded by three cranes. The haiku poem above depicts the miraculous appearance of Tridamos (as an auroch) on the edge of ploughed fields illuminated by the warmth of the rising sun. The auroch (*Bos primigenius*) is a species of wild ox which has been extinct for several centuries. It is thought that domestic cattle are probably descended from the auroch. The aurochs were black, stood 1.8 metres high at the shoulder, and had spreading, forward-curving horns. In Classical Antiquity, aurochs populated both Britain and Gaul, and they were described by Julius Caesar as follows:

"They are slightly smaller than elephants, and in appearance, colour, and shape they resemble bulls. They are extremely fierce and swift-footed and attack people and animals on sight. The Germans carefully trap them in pits and then slaughter them. Such tasks make the young German men tough, and this type of hunting gives them training. Those who kill the most wild oxen display the horns in public as a proof, which wins them considerable acclaim. The oxen cannot grow accustomed to people, or become tame, even if they are caught when young. The size, appearance, and shape of their horns are very different from the horns of our own cattle. These horns are much prized: the Germans give them a rim of silver and use them as drinking-vessels at magnificent feasts."[15]

---

15   J. Caesar, *The Gallic War*, 6.28.

Niskus

The scarlet-streaked sky —
as the thief drowns in the mere
silver coins flow out

Commentary

In ancient Romano-British religion, Niskus was an obscure deity, who appears to have been a tutelary god of the River Hamble in Hampshire, southern England. He is attested in only one inscription on a lead course tablet. It was found in 1982 in Badnam Creek, a tributary of River Hamble. The artefact is dated to about 350 or 400 CE, and it was offered by Muconius, a man — probably a merchant — angry at the mystery thief who stole his gold and silver coins. Curse tablets were inscribed pieces of lead used for asking a deity for favours, usually the restitution of stolen goods and punishing the perpetrators of the crime. The heavy, cold, and dull nature of lead also made it the perfect medium for inscribed curses because such attributes, generally associated with lifelessness, were thought to be transferable to the targeted individuals. Though the identity of Niskus is uncertain, some scholars have suggested that the deity may have been a male version of Niska, the Gaulish water-nymphs associated with the hot spring at Aix-les-Bains in France.

The haiku poem above depicts the punishment inflicted by Niskus on the thief who robbed Muconius. The sky suddenly becomes blood-red, indicating that justice is about to be served. The criminal slips into the lake and is dragged down by a supernatural force, malevolent water-nymphs ruled by Niskus. Upon the ruffian's drowning, the stolen property miraculously flows out onto the surface of the pond.

Apollo Cunomaglus

Black hounds chase the deer
deep in the shady thicket;
rising crescent moon

Commentary

In the religion of the ancient Britons, Cunomaglus was a deity associated with hunting, forests, and healing. His name meant "Hound Lord" in Brythonic. In the Roman period, he was syncretised with Apollo. Cunomaglus is attested on one inscription at Nettleton Shrub in Wiltshire, where he was worshipped along with Diana, Silvanus, Mars, and Rosmerta.

The haiku poem above, set during the Roman occupation of Britain, depicts a dynamic hunting scene taking place somewhere near Nettleton Shrub.

Abandinus

The sun's blazing eyes
gaze into the chilly spring
where clouds and leaves swim

Commentary

In the Romano-British religion, Abandinus was an obscure deity worshipped in the fort of Durovigutum in Cambridgeshire (in present-day Godmanchester). The god is attested only on one inscription, an inscribed bronze feather, very likely some votive object dedicated to him. Abandinus was possibly associated with either a natural spring or a stream in the vicinity of the fort.

The haiku poem above depicts above depicts the warm September sun breaking through the clouds to shine into the holy well dedicated to Abandinus.

Arnemetia

As the pearl clouds swirl
mellow light fills the temple
amid falling leaves

Commentary

In the Romano-British religion, Arnemetia was a goddess worshipped at the spa of *Aquae Arnemetiae* ("Waters of Arnemetia"), which is the present-day town of Buxton in north-west Derbyshire. The name of the deity means "she who dwells in the sacred grove". It has been suggested that prior to Roman occupation, the Corieltauvi tribe of the region worshipped the goddess in a grove near the hot spring.

The haiku poem above, set sometime during Roman period, depicts late afternoon sunlight pouring into the temple of Arnemetia.

Cuda

Slowly flowing creek
snakes through the serene valley
where sheep drowse in warmth

Commentary

Cuda was an obscure Romano-British goddess worshipped primarily in the Cotswolds. In one of his papers, Stephen Yeates has examined the toponymic evidence linked to the word Cotswold and suggested a possible relationship with the goddess Cuda.[16] In 1951, a votive relief inscribed with the name of the goddess was uncovered in a field in Daglingworth near Cirencester. The relief depicts a seated mother-goddess accompanied by three standing hooded male figures, who are known by scholars as the *genii cucullati*.

The haiku poem above depicts a typical Cotswolds landscape of rolling hills and valleys, pastures, and farmed slopes. During the middle ages, the Cotswolds became prosperous from the wool trade with the continent due to the productive local breed of sheep; much of the money made from wool was directed towards the building of churches.

---

16   S. Yeates, *The Cotswolds, the Codeswellan, and the Goddess Cuda*, 2004.

Viridius

Though snow starts to flake
the green god's moss-covered head
peers out of the grove

Commentary

In the religion of ancient Britain, Viridius (or Viridios) was a regional god, who appears to have been worshipped in what is now Lincolnshire. Two inscribed stones dedicated to him were discovered in Ancaster. The etymology of his name ("mighty, virile, verdant, fertile") suggests that Viridius might have been a vegetation deity, embodying the growth cycle of plants. He bears a certain resemblance to the Green Man, a ubiquitous medieval motif of a head crowned with leaves and vines.

A curious limestone figurative carving, probably utilised as an altarpiece, was also found near Ancaster. The object was dated to the late Iron Age. The carving represents a naked man holding an axe and standing beneath an archway. There are no inscriptions on the stone. Yet the location of the find near Ancaster and the features displayed on the god have led some scholars to hypothesise that the altarpiece is a depiction of Viridius.

The haiku poem above depicts the appearance of Viridius in a thicket near Ancaster. It is already late November and the first heavy snow of the year has started to fall. Yet the green figure symbolises the eternal truth that winter will not last forever, that spring will bring the cycle of new growth. The snow will eventually melt, the flowers on the meadows will bloom once again, and the bird songs will echo in the lush woods.

PART FIVE

NORTHERN BRITAIN

Coventina

A small bell tingles —
one red leaf falls from the elm
to the glassy well

Commentary

In the Romano-British religion, Coventina was a goddess associated with wells and springs. She is attested on fourteen inscriptions found on the site of a Roman fort and settlement called Brocolita (possibly meaning "badger holes"), present-day Carrawburgh in Northumberland. Instead of the central sanctuary or *cella* which would be expected in a Roman temple, a small enclosure containing a well was found on the site. Numerous votive figures and gifts were discovered in the well, as well as about 13,000 coins. The soldiers stationed at Brocolita were Batavians, and several individuals who are named in the inscriptions came from around the modern Dutch Rhine delta. Coventina was generally portrayed as a water nymph and is called *nimpha* in one inscription.

The haiku poem above, set during a cloudy October day, depicts an imaginary synchronicity taking place in Coventina's sanctuary at Brocolita. As the priest rings the bell, a solitary leaf falls from the nearby tree and is carried by the wind straight into the sacred well. Many Romano-British temple sites contained small copper-alloy or iron bells, which were rung during religious ceremonies.[17]

---

17   Eckardt, H. and S. Williams, 2018, *The Sound of Magic? Bells in Roman Britain*, *Britannia* 49, 179–210.

Vernostonus

Catkins in the wind —
the grim groaning of alder trunks
near carved altar stones

Commentary

In the religion of ancient Britain, Vernostonus was a deity associated with alder trees. In etymological terms, it has been suggested that his name may be derived from the Proto-Celtic *Werno-stonos*, meaning "the groaning of alder-trunks". An inscription dedicated to Vernostonus was recovered at the Roman fort of Vindomara (present-day Ebchester). Sometimes he is perceived as an epithet of Cocidius, a well-attested Romano-British deity associated with war and hunting.

Alder trees are usually found near streams, rivers, and wetlands. With a few exceptions, alders are deciduous, and the leaves are alternate, simple, and serrated. The flowers are catkins; male catkins are elongated while the female ones are short and round. They are mainly pollinated by wind, though sometimes they also attract bees. Both male and female catkins develop in autumn and remain dormant during winter. The common alder is vital to wildlife all year round. Its seeds are good winter food for birds. Deer, sheep, hares, and rabbits feed on the tree, and it provides shelter for livestock in winter. It shades the water of rivers and streams, decreasing the water temperature. This is particularly important for fish which also find safety among its exposed roots in times of flood.

De Excidio et Conquestu Britanniae

Swarms of wicked worms
emerge from strait crevices;
Hadrian's wall at night

Approaching warships —
wolves break into the sheepfold
unclosed by herdsmen

Commentary

De Excidio et Conquestu Britanniae ("On the Ruin and Conquest of Britain") is the title of a work written in Latin by the 6th-century British cleric St Gildas. It is a sermon that consists of three parts: a historical preface, a complaint against the sub-Roman rulers, and a critique of the British clergy.

The preface is a selective recounting of events during the Roman occupation and subsequent withdrawal of Britain whose purpose is to illustrate the wicked behaviour of the Britons that led to their demise. According to Leslie Alcock, Gildas "tells us a great deal about both the political arrangements and ecclesiastical organisation of western Britain in the sixth century".[18]

The haiku poems above were inspired by the following passages from *De Excidio*. They refer to Pictish and Scottish raids on Britain and the invitation of Anglo-Saxon mercenaries to deal with the former, respectively:

"As [the Romans] were returning home, the terrible hordes of Scots and Picts eagerly come forth out of the tiny boats in which they sailed across

---

18   L. Alcock, *Arthur's Britain*, p. 29.

the sea-valley, as on Ocean's deep, just as, when the sun is high and the heat increasing, **dark swarms of worms emerge from the narrow crevices of their holes**".[19]

"Then all the councillors, together with that proud tyrant Vortigern, the British king, were so blinded, that, as a protection to their country, they sealed its doom **by inviting in among them like wolves into the sheep-fold**, the fierce and impious Saxons, a race hateful both to God and men, to repel the invasions of the northern nations".[20]

---

19   Gildas, *De Excidio et Conquestu Britanniae*, chapter 19.

20   *Ibid.*, chapter 23.

Condatis

Where the rivers meet
weary merchants offer milk
at the islet's shrine

Commentary

In the religion of the ancient Celts, Condatis was a deity associated with the confluences of rivers. His name is thought to have been derived from the Proto-Celtic *kom-dātī, meaning "confluence," a meeting of waters. He appears to have been worshipped in northern Britain, for archaeological evidence of his veneration is found mostly in County Durham. A single inscription dedicated to him was found in north-western Gaul, however. In the *interpretatio romana*, he was syncretised with Mars.

The haiku poem above depicts a shrine to Condatis, located on a small islet near the confluence of the River Wear and the Cong Burn, east of Chester-le-Street in County Durham. As an expression of their gratitude for safe and unhindered travel, foreign merchants make an offering to Condatis.

Brigantia

Crowning at the heights — empyrean beams of splendour peer through amber clouds

Commentary

In the religion of the ancient Celts, Brigantia was a goddess worshipped primarily in northern Britain and southern Scotland. The name of the deity means "the exalted one". Brigantia appears to have been the goddess of the Brigantes, a powerful northern British tribal confederacy. The Greek geographer Ptolemy placed another tribe of the same name in the extreme south-east of Ireland. However, it is not clear what connection, if any, existed between the Irish and the British Brigantes.

According to Ptolemy, the territory of the British Brigantes stretched from the North Sea to the Irish Sea. Their heartland seems to have been what was later called Yorkshire. It has been suggested that the Brigantes occupied the elevated hillforts in the Pennines, from which they launched attacks on their neighbours. The Brigantes were particularly troublesome to the Romans. Initially, they actively resisted attempts to be conquered. In later years, they frequently rebelled to throw off Roman rule or showed signs of unrest.

Toponymic studies have shown multiple place names across Continental Europe that derive from *Brigantium*, the neuter form of the same adjective of which the feminine became the name of the goddess Brigantia. That being the case, the connection of these places with the goddess is dubious, because the toponyms are easily explained as referring to a "high fort" or "high place" in the literal sense. Some scholars have also attempted to associate Brigantia with the Irish characters of Brigit and Saint Brigid. These parallels, however close they may seem at first glance, are not established as a fact and are open to debate.[21]

The haiku poem above depicts the coronation rites of a Brigantian king on one October day. Blessed by the celestial rays of the goddess Brigantia, it seems that the king's reign will be long and prosperous.

---

21   L. M. Bitel, *St. Brigit of Ireland: From Virgin Saint to Fertility Goddess*, 2001.

Setlocenia

Seashore bathed in gold —
the frail crone's silent prayer
makes the pale sun stay

Commentary

Setlocenia was a minor goddess of early northern Britain. An altar dedicated to her was found at Maryport in Cumbria. The name of the deity may have been derived from the Proto-Celtic *saytlo* meaning "lifetime" and *keno* meaning "long". Therefore, it has been suggested that Setlocenia might have been a goddess of longevity worshipped by the Cumbrian Carvetii. The Carvetii were one of the many smaller tribes that made up the Brigantian confederation of northern England. Their name is usually translated as "those who belong to the deer". They occupied the extreme north-west corner of Brigantian territory, comprising what is now Cumberland and part of Westmorland. The capital of the Carvetii is presumed to have been Luguvalium (Carlisle), the only walled town known in the region.

The haiku poem above, set in October, depicts an elderly Carvetian woman standing at the seashore near present-day Maryport. Being a devotee of Setlocenia, she offers her respectful obeisances to the deity. Though the days are already cold and short, Setlocenia makes the pale sun set a little later than usual.

Mars Belatucadros

Besieged fort at dawn —
a tall, lustrous champion
slays the dark-haired foe

Commentary

Belatucadros was a deity venerated in northern Celtic Britain, especially in what is now Cumberland and Westmorland. In the *interpretatio romana*, Belatucadros was syncretised with Mars. Altars consecrated to him were usually small and plain, leading to the suggestion that he was worshipped by lower-ranked Roman soldiers as well as by native Britons. The majority of inscriptions dedicated to Belatucadros occur near Hadrian's Wall. His name is usually translated as "fair shining one" or "fair slayer".

The haiku poem above, set in the 4th century, depicts a Roman fort assaulted by the Picts. Due to the lack of raids in recent years, discipline and vigilance among Roman soldiers on the frontier have become lax. Their great devotion to Belatucadros makes up for these deficits. Miraculously, the fair-haired deity appears for a moment in the gate of the fortress. His lustrous presence makes the Picts tremble in fear and lose their courage, especially when Belatucadros kills their chieftain.

Ricagambeda

Blazing gloaming falls —
the bow ard drawn by oxen
turns up a carved stone

Commentary

Ricagambeda was a Celtic goddess worshipped in Roman Britain. She is attested in a single inscription on an altar stone found at Birrens (the Roman fort of Blatobulgium) in what is now Dumfries, Scotland. The object is dated to the period between 155 and 180 CE. The Latin inscription states that the altar was erected by men from the Vellavian district serving in the Second Cohort of Tungrians in fulfilment of a vow to the goddess. It has been suggested that the deity's name may be related to the Gaulish word *ricā, meaning "furrow". Thus, Ricagambeda may have been an agricultural goddess of fertility and abundance.

The haiku poem above depicts the moment when a similar carved stone dedicated to Ricagambeda was accidentally unearthed by a farmer's bow ard (a type of primitive plough). It is a well-known fact that ploughing in late autumn allows the frost to till the ground. In the Celtic Iron Age, this agricultural practice was done using the simple iron-shod crook or bow ard, which cut a furrow in the soil. The field was ploughed in two directions at right angles, to break up the ground sufficiently for sowing.[22] Historically, the first ploughs were devoid of wheels, but Celtic peoples began utilising wheeled ploughs during the Roman era.

---

22   B. Cunliffe, *Iron Age Communities in Britain* (London: Routledge, 2005), p. 413.

Scotti

Grim dawn at the shore —
sea marauders seize the fort
where bribed sentries sleep

Commentary

Scotti (or Scoti) was a Latin name for the Gaels, first attested in the late 3rd century CE. The term was mainly used to describe Gaelic population groups that launched attacks on Roman Britain. The incursions had become more severe from 367 CE when the Scotti conspired with the Picts and Saxons and launched simultaneously coordinated attacks on Roman outposts and towns. Roman military intelligence (the *areani*) that provided information on enemy movements was bribed to keep silent, allowing the invaders to have the advantage of surprise. Deserting Roman soldiers and escaped slaves roamed the countryside and turned to robbery to support themselves. Although the chaos was widespread and initially collective, the goals of the rebels were merely personal enrichment, and they worked as small bands rather than larger armies. Eventually, Count Theodosius dealt with the invaders and restored order the following year.

The haiku poem above, set in 367 CE, depicts a Roman promontory fort in north-western Britain, one of many that fell to barbarian raids that year. Having bribed the local sentries, Gaelic raiders descend upon the shore and take the fortress by surprise.

Llywarch Hen

September has come —
when I stroll down the steep hill
chill strikes my frail bones

Commentary

Llywarch Hen ("Llywarch the Old") was an early medieval Cumbric bard and prince. Along with his contemporaries Taliesin, Aneirin, and Myrddin, he is regarded to be one of the four great bards of early Welsh poetry. Though it is unknown whether he actually wrote the poems attributed to him, he is believed to have been a historical person living in the 6th century. Llywarch Hen was the cousin of the famous king Urien of Rheged. Following the death of Urien, he was forced to flee to the court of Cynddylan in the Kingdom of Powys. When Cynddylan was slain in battle, Llywarch was left friendless and indigent, with nothing but the milk from a single cow to feed him. Legend has it that he moved to a remote hut at Aber Ciog in North Wales, where he spent the rest of his days composing some of the most beautiful verses found in early Welsh poetry.

According to *Bonedd Gwŷr y Gogledd* ("The Descent of the Men of the North", a genealogical tract written in Middle Welsh), he was around eighty years old at the time of his death, in keeping with his epithet "the Old". However, other sources provide different birth and death dates, with claims of his age reaching 105, or even 150 years.

Cataractonium

Crows perch on the mounds
where mead-nurtured men fell;
slow falls softly sough

Commentary

Catterick is a village and civil parish in North Yorkshire, England. According to one possible etymological interpretation, the name of the village is derived from the Latin place name *Cataractonium*, meaning "place of a waterfall". Alternatively, *Cataractonium* might have been a Roman misunderstanding of the Celtic toponym *Catu-rātis*, meaning "battle ramparts". Catterick is thought to have been the site of the Battle of Catraeth.

In the post-Roman period, Gododdin (Old Welsh *Guotodin*) was a Brythonic kingdom in south-east Scotland. The name derives from the Votadini, an earlier tribal group which lived in the same region. The deeds of the men of Gododdin are praised in *Y Gododdin*, an early medieval Welsh epic poem describing the Battle of Catraeth, which was fought around 600 CE between them and the Angles of Bernicia and Deira. After a year of feasting at Din Eydin, present-day Edinburgh, the men of Gododdin assembled a host and rode to face the Angles. The Britons were utterly crushed, and out of all the warriors who went to Catraeth, the only one who returned alive was the bard Aneirin, who composed the elegiac poem in question.

The haiku poem above depicts the imaginary burial mounds of Brythonic warriors who fell at Catraeth. Despite the gloomy atmosphere of the knolls, softly soughing waterfalls on the nearby River Swale bring an air of pastoral tranquillity. The poem also alludes to a famous passage from *Y Goddodin*: *he fed black ravens on the rampart of a fortress, though he was no Arthur*. These stanzas are thought to contain one of the first historical references to Arthur, a legendary British leader.

Yan Tan Tethera

Autumn departures —
the bedridden shepherd sighs
when ewes bleat feebly

Commentary

Yan Tan Tethera is a sheep-counting system traditionally used by shepherds in Northern England and earlier in some other parts of Britain. Until the Industrial Revolution, the employment of traditional numerical systems was widespread among shepherds, notably in the remote fells of the Lake District. These numbers were used in children's counting games, to count sheep and cattle, knitting stitches, and money. Like traditional Welsh numbers, the sheep scoring systems are vigesimal (based on the number twenty, unlike the decimal system).

Some scholars argue that *Yan Tan Tethera* contains genuine traces of the extinct Cumbric language. It is thought that Cumbric fell out of use in the 12th century when the Kingdom of Strathclyde was annexed to Scotland. The Gaelicisation of this region proceeded most swiftly among the former Brythonic elites because all social advancement depended on an ability to speak Gaelic.[23] The remains of Cumbric, however, may have lingered for quite some time in the memory of rural people, as the instance of *Yan Tan Tethera* indicates.

The haiku poem above depicts an elderly shepherd from the Lake District. Bedridden (and possibly on the verge of dying) in a *shieling*, he is unable to take proper care of his herd. A *shieling* is a roughly constructed hut used by shepherds tending cattle or sheep on the high or remote ground. In general, these mountain shelters became abandoned by the end of the 17th century, although in some areas this system continued into the

---

23   T. Clarkson, *The Men of the North* (Edinburgh: Birlinn, 2010), p. 195-196.

next centuries. The word *shieling* also refers to the practice of transhumance, a seasonal movement of livestock between higher pastures in summer and lower valleys in late autumn. *Autumn departures* in the first line of the poem, allude, in a figurative sense, to the extinction of the *Yan Tan Tethera* sheep scoring system. With the shepherd's passing, his children will no longer know how to count livestock in this traditional manner.

The Assasination of Urien Rheged

The owl's doomy hoot —
brief flash in the looking glass
on a starless night

Though bloodstains are cleared
his hair turns white overnight;
stormy sea at dawn

Commentary

Urien Rheged was a late 6th-century king of Rheged, the post-Roman kingdom in northern Britain and southern Scotland. Urien was one of the most renowned early medieval Brythonic monarchs. His military deeds are widely celebrated in Old Welsh poetry. He and his son Owain were also incorporated into Arthurian legend.

Around 580 CE, Urien initiated a campaign against the Angles of Deira and Bernicia. In traditional interpretation, he led a coalition of northern kingdoms, gathering Rhydderch Hael of Alt Clut, Gwallawc Marchawc Trin of Elmet, Morcant Bulc of Bryneich, and Áedán mac Gabráin of Dál Riada. The coalition won a series of victories: Gwen Ystrad, Berwyn, and Argoed Llywfein where Owain was supposed to have killed Theodoric, the Angle king. Finally, Urien and his allies besieged the Angles at the tidal island of Lindisfarne, which was then known as *Ynis Metcaud*.[24] However, a man called Llofan Llaf Difo ("Severing-Hand") is said to have assassinated Urien at the instigation of Morcant Bulc. The latter was jealous

---

24   It is thought that the old Welsh name *Ynys Medcaut* is derived from the Latin *Insula Medicata*, referring to the medicinal properties of herbs found there. For more information about the island's rich history, please refer to: A. Moffat, *To the Island of Tides: A Journey to Lindisfarne* (Edinburgh: Canongate Books, 2019).

of Urien, whose military skill and generalship surpassed that of all the other kings. According to tradition, the murder took place when Urien was on an expedition at Aber Lleu.

The first haiku poem above illustrates omens preceding the assassination of Urien Rheged. An owl's hoot in the nearby copse conveys a sense of foreboding doom. As the poem suggests, the flash in the hand-mirror does not refer to nocturnal light of the moon or stars. Instead, it alludes to the glint of Llofan's dagger.

The second poem was inspired by David Lynch's *Twin Peaks*, as well as William Shakespeare's tragedy *Macbeth*. Having killed Urien, Llofan Llaf Difo manages to escape. He takes a short bath in the sea to remove all traces of blood from his body and clothes. Satisfied with the outcome, the hireling returns to Morcant's encampment to claim the reward for successful assassination. However, in a miraculous event, Llofan's hair turns white overnight, clearly indicating his guilt. Later Welsh poetry will condemn the murderer, calling the death of Urien one of the "Three Unfortunate Assassinations".

Din Rheged

Sombre court at night —
snell wind whistles through loose planks
where noctules roost now

Commentary

Dunragit is a hamlet between Stranraer and Glenluce in Dumfries and Galloway, south-west Scotland. According to one possible interpretation, the toponym Dunragit is derived from *Din Rheged* meaning "Fort of Rheged", alluding to the Brythonic kingdom of Rheged which flourished in northern Britain between the fifth and seventh centuries. It is possible that this was one of the royal sites used by the kings of Rheged, and it has been further suggested as the site of King Arthur's northern court, *Pen Rhionydd*, recorded in the medieval *Welsh Triads*. Contrarily, others have hypothesised that the second element could be the Gaelic *reichet* rather than the Old Welsh *reget*, and that the place was so named by the *Gall-Goídil*, "foreign Gaels", who colonised Galloway in the Viking period.[25]

The haiku poem above attempts to find an intermediate position between these two conflicting theories. Set sometime in the 8th century, it depicts a dilapidated fortified settlement at Din Rheged. In this interpretation, the fort was occupied in the late 6th century by a minor nobleman from the kingdom of Rheged. It has never been a significant site, however. Din Rheged had already been abandoned by the time Northumbrians advanced into Galloway in the second half of the 7th century. It has been suggested that the betrothal of Oswiu, King of Northumbria, to Rieinmelth, the great-granddaughter and only remaining heiress of Urien of Rheged, brought Galloway into Northumbrian sovereignty relatively peacefully. The marriage, which probably took place in 638, may have advanced Northumbria's expansion westward. Rieinmelth's

---

25   T. Clarkson, *The Men of the North*, p. 71.

position as the surviving inheritress to the kings of Rheged appears to indicate that the males of the princely line were dead and the resistance broken by the time the marriage was arranged.[26]

The common noctule (*Nyctalus noctula*), depicted in the poem, is a species of insectivorous bat. The noctule has vivid, golden-brown fur, with darker wings, ears, and face. Its flight is swift, reaching speeds of up to 50 km/h. These bats mainly consume beetles, moths, and winged ants. At the beginning of winter — usually in November, although this greatly depends on the ambient temperatures, they start to hibernate in large groups with both sexes in one roost. Tree holes are not warm enough, so they seek caves, abandoned buildings, and church steeples.

---

26   *Ibid.* p. 125.

Saint Ninian's Cave

The druid's long breath —
great primordial stillness
perfused with soft breeze

Sounds of crashing waves
pierce the horrible blackness
of this deep, dank cave

Ancient cave carvings
defaced by a zealous monk;
rock slide shuts him in

Commentary

Ninian is a Christian saint first mentioned in the 8th century by Bede the Venerable as being an early missionary among the Picts of southern Scotland. For this reason, he is often referred to as the *Apostle to the Southern Picts*. Ninian's main shrine was at Whithorn in Galloway, where he erected a small stone church known as the *Candida Casa*. The church site quickly grew to prominence in the early medieval period, becoming a cathedral and monastery, and remaining a centre for pilgrimage despite the unstable political situation in the region.

Saint Ninian's Cave, situated a few kilometres from Whithorn Abbey, is traditionally believed to have been a place of retreat for Saint Ninian. The holy man was said to *study heavenly wisdom with a devoted mind in a place of horrible blackness*. According to another theory, the cave could have been a chapel or stone-carving workshop. Archaeological excavations uncovered a collection of early medieval carved stones. There were eighteen in total, most of them built into a post-medieval wall, others lying loose in the cave's interior or at its mouth. In 1884, a skeleton was found buried in the outer part of the cave. The burial was possibly that of a hermit, who had retreated to the cave, with a cross later set up to mark his grave.[27]

The haiku triad above utilises elements of poetic license. However, it does not depict something implausible — the cave might have been used long before the arrival of Christianity in southern Scotland. In the first poem, a Pictish druid is seen meditating there. A few centuries later, a Christian zealot destroys pagan carvings on the cave's wall. When he is about to leave, a sudden cave-in blocks the outer passage, and the monk's fanaticism is punished — unable to escape, he will probably starve to death.

---

27   C. A. R. Radford, *Excavations at Whithorn (final report)*, Transactions and Journal of Proceedings Dumfriesshire and Galloway Natural History and Antiquarian Society, 3rd, vol. 34, 1955-6.

Ynis Manaw

Mildewed dock cellar
swarms with anurous longtails;
odd sound of tapping

Commentary

On the Isle of Man (*Ynis Manaw* in Welsh), *longtail* is a euphemism used to denote a rat. According to a relatively modern superstition, saying the word "rat" is believed to bring bad luck. The roots of this custom can be traced back to sea-taboos, where specific phrases were not uttered aboard ship, for fear of attracting bad luck or bad weather.

The haiku poem above depicts a damp cellar in the docks, which is full of tailless (anurous) rats. The dominant trait of taillessness, which characterises some mammals (such as cats) from the Isle of Man, results from a spontaneous mutation, the Manx taillessness gene, that eventually became common on the island due to the limited genetic diversity.

The poem was inspired by *The Rats in the Walls*, a short story written by H. P. Lovecraft.

PART SIX

SCOTLAND

Clota

Sussurous white cloots —
auburn leaves hide the brock's sett
bathed in mellow light

Commentary

In Celtic mythology, Clota is the reconstructed name of the tutelary deity of the River Clyde in southern Scotland. The earliest written record for the River Clyde is from Tacitus, who lists it as *Clōta*. Writing in the 7th century, Adomnán records it as *Clōithe*. According to W. J. Watson, the name refers to a hypothetical goddess, **Clōta*, whose name means "the washer, the strongly flowing one". The scholar also notes that the nearby river Cart, which flows into Clyde, is connected with the Irish verb *cartaim*, "I cleanse".[28] Folk belief has it that the waters of Clyde are thought to be useful in controlling seizures.

The haiku poem above refers to the Falls of Clyde, the collective name of four spectacular waterfalls on the River Clyde near New Lanark in Lanarkshire. Providing a suitable habitat for many species, the woodlands surrounding the falls are rich in wildlife. Badgers, otters, roe deer, bats, and over one hundred species of birds (including a resident pair of nesting peregrine falcons) have been recorded to live in this area.

Badgers (also known as brocks) are omnivorous mammals with large black-and-white facial stripes. These nocturnal animals are equipped with short legs and sharp claws by nature, which are ideal for digging. Badgers create extensive underground dwellings called setts, with tunnels connecting chambers that are lined with dry bedding material such as grass, moss, and bracken.

---

28   W. J. Watson, *The Celtic Place-names of Scotland* (Edinburgh: Birlinn, 1993), p. 44.

Clooties are holy wells or springs, almost always with a tree growing beside them, where strips of cloth or rags have been left, usually tied to the branches of the tree as part of a healing ritual. In Scots, a "clootie" or "cloot" is also a term for a strip of cloth or rag.

I dedicate this poem to my friend Adam who is a great lover of badgers.

Antonine Wall

The crumbling earthwork
winds through the craggy upland;
weathered stones at dusk

Commentary

The Antonine Wall was an earthwork fortification on stone foundations, built by Romans in Scotland. The wall, located between the Firth of Forth and the Firth of Clyde, was erected in the years after 142 CE during the reign of emperor Antoninus Pius. Its purpose was to protect the northernmost frontier barrier of the Roman Empire against the intrusions of Caledonian tribes. The fortification spanned approximately sixty-three kilometres and stood about three metres high and five metres wide. Furthermore, sixteen forts and many smaller fortlets were set up along the wall. All were connected by a road known as the Military Way. After only twenty years, however, the Antonine Wall was abandoned as the imperial frontier retreated south to Hadrian's Wall.

The haiku poem above depicts the remains of the wall, a few centuries after it was abandoned by the Romans.

Beinn Laomainn

The beacons are lit!
snekkjas approach the crannog
swathed in drowsiness

Commentary

Beinn Laomainn is the Scottish Gaelic name for Ben Lomond, a prominent mountain in the Scottish Highlands. The peak is located on the eastern shore of Loch Lomond. The name *Bein Laomainn* is usually translated as "Beacon Mountain" or "Beacon Hill". Thus, Ben Lomond was probably a beacon mountain where warning fires were lit if hostile ships were spotted in the lake below.

The setting of the poem is a misty September morning in 1263. It is said that in this year Magnús Óláfsson, the Hiberno-Norse king of Mann and the Isles, carried out a raid into Loch Lomond, plundering settlements on the lake's shores. The attack took place during the Norwegian expedition to Scotland, whose goal was to resolve the dispute over the ownership of the Hebrides.

The Norwegian overlordship over the Hebrides had been contested since the 1240s, when the Scottish king, Alexander II, began asking King Haakon IV of Norway if he could purchase the islands from him. For almost a decade these efforts were unsuccessful, and the negotiations ceased for thirteen years after Alexander II died. When his son Alexander III came to power in 1262, he sent Haakon a final request declaring that if Haakon did not sell him the Islands they would take them by force. In response, Haakon gathered a fleet of over 120 warships and sailed out in July 1263 to re-assert Norwegian control along the western seaboard of Scotland.

The previously-mentioned Magnús Óláfsson was Haakon's ally and vassal. The Norwegian king ordered Magnús and his Hiberno-Norse allies to attack the district of Lennox. According to *The Saga of Haakon Haakonarson*, after dragging their vessels overland from the nearby Loch Long, Magnús and his comrades launched their ships from what is today Tarbet and pillaged the islands and shores of Loch Lomond. The ships utilised in the raid must have been *snekkjas* — vessels lighter and smaller than famous *drakkars*.

Crannogs were artificial islands built on lakes, rivers, and estuarine waters of Ireland, Scotland, and Wales. Crannog construction and occupation was at its peak in Scotland from about 800 BCE to 200 CE. There is no doubt that these artificial islets offered a substantial degree of protection from wild animals and were easily defensible in case of raids. That being the case, most crannogs seem to have been built as individual dwellings to accommodate extended families. They could be accessed either by a bridge or by coracles and dugout canoes. The specific crannog in the poem was known as Clàr-Innis. It was built on a flat island in the eastern part of Loch Lomond. Clàr-Innis was the seat of Clan Buchanan at the time of the raid.

The Viking ships launched at Tarbet were most likely seen from the top of Ben Lomond, where a warning beacon was lit. Ben Lomond is visible from Conic Hill, a prominent hill close to the crannog at Clàr-Innis. Therefore, its dwellers, warned by the chain of lit beacons, could probably prepare themselves for the raid.

Fartairchill

The vile oorlich thief
lurks behind the ancient yew;
kirk wrapped in dawn's haze

Commentary

Fartairchill is the Scottish Gaelic name for Fortingall, a small village in Perthshire, Scotland. The name of the settlement means "church at the foot of an escarpment". The place is famous for its ancient yew tree, growing near the modern parish church. Thought to be at least 2000 years old, it is one of the oldest trees in Britain. The nearby Christian temple, on the other hand, is built on an early medieval monastic site, probably founded about 700 CE. Crop-marks of surrounding trenched enclosures have been identified from the air, and fragments of some intricately carved Pictish cross-slabs preserved in the church all point to an early origin as a significant church site.

Moreover, an early hand-bell in Irish style (dating from the 7th or 8th century) used to be stored in an alcove in the church. The instrument, meant to be hit with a metal rod, was made of iron coated with bronze. However, the bell was stolen in 2017. The bell may have belonged to Saint Adomnán, the biographer of Saint Columba, who came to the area from Iona as a missionary of the Columban church.

The setting of the haiku poem above is a rainy September morning in 2017 when the hand-bell was stolen.

The Scottish National Dictionary defines the adjective *oorlich* as "miserable-looking from cold, hunger or illness, pinched, haggard, shivery, out-of-sorts".

Càrn na Marbh

When the first snow flakes
the Samhnag lit on the mound
flickers and dies out

Commentary

Càrn na Marbh had originally been a Bronze Age tumulus. It was re-used in the second half of the 14th century for burying victims of the Black Death away from the church graveyard at Fortingall. An upright boulder known as *Clach a' Phlàigh*, "the Plague Stone", stands at the top of the mound. A tablet on the stone is engraved with the words:

Here lie the victims of the Great Plague of the 14th Century, taken here on a sledge drawn by a white horse led by an old woman.

Until 1924, *Càrn na Marbh* was the focal point of an ancient Samhain festival. A great bonfire or *Samhnag* was lit on the top of it each year. The whole community climbed the hill and danced round the mound both sunwise (*deiseil*) and against the sun (*tuathal*). As the fire began to die, the boys took burning embers from the flames and ran throughout the field with them, finally throwing them into the air and dancing over them as they lay glowing on the ground. At the very end, the young men leapt across the remains of the bonfire, following the footsteps of their ancient Celtic ancestors who had believed in the purificatory power of fire.[29]

---

29   A. Moffat, *The Faded Map: Lost Kingdoms of Scotland* (Edinburgh: Birlinn, 2011), p. 225.

Sluagh

At the dead of night
the west window flings open
though the air is still

Commentary

In Irish and Scottish folklore, the *Sluagh* (meaning "the horde" or "the host") are said to be spirits of the restless dead. Sometimes they are perceived as criminals or generally wicked people who were rejected by both the afterlife and the earth. These creatures are almost always portrayed as troublesome and malevolent. They were seen to fly in groups like flocks of birds, arriving from the west, and were feared for their habit of entering the house of a dying person to carry the soul away with them. Traditionally, west-facing windows were sometimes kept shut to keep them out. It seems that the *Sluagh* also harassed the living. According to Alexander Carmichael, they carried humans off into the skies, returning them "exhausted and prostrate".

The haiku poem above depicts the arrival of the *Sluagh* in a house where someone has recently passed away.

Dun Durn

An old buzzard's call
above the montane fastness;
hazy gloaming falls

Commentary

The haiku poem above refers to Dun Durn, the site of a large Pictish hillfort, located at the western end of Strathearn in Perth and Kinross, Scotland. The evidence from archaeological excavations suggests that the main entrance to the fort was situated on the west side of the hill. A precipitous path snaked around the outer ramparts, then passed through a gate, and continued to wind its way in a spiral, up and around the hill, until it reached the small, circular summit. A timber-laced stone fortress stood there, though it is unclear whether a roof covered it. The courtyard beneath it, which formed the main enclosure of the fort, contained a well and domestic buildings. A significant amount of metalwork, leatherwork, and glass was excavated on the site, which shows that during the early medieval period Dun Durn was an important stronghold. It likely protected the western borders of the Pictish kingdom against the encroachment of Dál Riadan Scots.[30]

Dun Durn is mentioned twice in historical documents. According to the *Annals of Ulster*, the fastness was besieged in 683 CE by an unknown hostile force, possibly Dal Riádan Scots. *The Scottish Regnal Lists* mention that King Girg, son of Dungal, died at Dun Durn in 889 CE.

---

30   A. Konstam, *Strongholds of the Picts* (Oxford: Osprey Publishing, 2010), p. 29-36.

Tuesis

Where the hawthorns grow
three ancient cairns fall apart;
yet turnstones stand still

Commentary

Tuesis was the name given by Ptolemy to a tribal settlement of the Vacomagi, who were an ancient people inhabiting the north-east of Scotland. This Greek geographer also mentioned the River Tuesis, which has now been identified with the River Spey. According to one possible etymological explanation (provided by W. J. Watson), the original meaning of the name Spey is "hawthorn stream".[31] In religious terms, it is likely that the Tuesis had its tutelary river goddess, perhaps of the same name.

The haiku poem above depicts a small islet on the river Spey. Something causes the old cairns to collapse, yet, as the third line suggests, the blame is not to be placed on the turnstones that happened to be near. Turnstones are two bird species of shorebirds: the ruddy turnstone (*Arenaria interpres*) and the black turnstone (*Arenaria melanocephala*). As the name implies, these birds use their short, flattened bills, which are slightly upturned at the tip, to overturn pebbles, shells, and seaweed in search of food. Turnstones grow to a length of about twenty centimetres.

The atmosphere of the poem was inspired by Jan Garbarek's song called *Where the Rivers Meet* (from the artist's album *Rites*).

---

31   W. J. Watson, *The Celtic Place-names of Scotland*, p. 474.

Glendaruel

The cuckoo's sweet song
as crimson clouds float gently;
wind on calm waters

Commentary

Glendaruel is the name of a glen — a deep, narrow valley — and a small river in the Cowal peninsula in Argyll, Scotland. According to W. J. Watson, the name Glendaruel means "glen of two red spots".[32] The place is thought to be *Glenn Dá Rúadh* found in the late medieval Gaelic poem *The Lament of Deirdre*. In the poem, Deirdre, a tragic heroine in Irish mythology, is lamenting the necessity of leaving Alba (Scotland) to return to Ireland. *The Lament of Deirdre* contains a reference to the sweet song of a cuckoo sitting on the bending tree above *Glenn Dá Rúadh*.

The haiku poem above depicts a fiery October twilight in Glendaruel. The atmosphere of the poem was inspired by *Wind on Water*, the introductory track from *Evening Star*, a collaborative album between Robert Fripp and Brian Eno.

---

32   W. J. Watson, *The Celtic Place-names of Scotland*, p. 474.

Loch Tatha

First light on the hills —
the merlin's flight through the loch
shrouded in dense mist

The sunless crannog —
leaves fall to the glassy loch
reflecting sunset

Dim light of the hearth —
the bridge creaks and groans loudly
in the dreich goselet

Commentary

Loch Tay (Scottish Gaelic: *Loch Tatha*) is a big freshwater lake in the
Central Highlands of Perthshire in Scotland.

Crannogs were artificial islands built on lakes, rivers, and estuarine
waters of Ireland, Scotland, and Wales. The construction and occupation of
crannogs was at its peak in Scotland from about 800 BCE to 200 CE. There
is no doubt that these artificial islets offered a substantial degree of
protection from wild animals and were easily defensible in case of raids.
That being the case, most crannogs seem to have been built as individual
dwellings to accommodate extended families. They could be accessed either
by a bridge or by coracles and dugout canoes.

The haiku triad above is a poetic depiction of different times of the day
at the reconstructed crannog at Loch Tay. The structure was built between
1994 and 1997 as an archaeological experiment led by Dr Nicholas Dixon

and Ms Barrie Andrian based on their underwater research.

The merlin is the smallest breeding falcon in Scotland and the British Isles. Despite their insignificant size, the merlins are skilled predators. Relying on speed and agility, they prey primarily on smaller birds such as the meadow pipit, skylark, and chaffinch. Where do the merlins go after the breeding season? Around late August or September, they tend to leave the uplands and move to lower altitudes. These include both coastal and farmland areas. Most Scottish merlins winter either in Scotland or England though some cross over to mainland Europe and ringed birds have been found as far south as Spain. Wintering merlins often prey on small wading birds in addition to the usual meadow pipits and other small passerine species. British merlins are joined in the winter by birds from Iceland.

The Scots word *dreich* means "bleak" or "cheerless" and is often used to describe typical Scottish weather. *The Scottish National Dictionary* defines the noun *goselet* as *a soaking, drenching, downpour (of rain)*.

Lavellan

Long trail of warm blood
leads to the deep noxious pool
where a dead calf lies

Commentary

In Scottish folklore, the lavellan is a mysterious cryptid (an animal whose existence or survival is disputed or unsubstantiated) from the Scottish Highlands. It is generally described as a furry rodent, larger than a rat, inhabiting deep pools in rivers. The breath of the creature is noxious; it is allegedly capable of injuring cattle from over thirty meters away. It is said that farmers kill lavellans on sight and preserve their skin because the water in which it has been dipped is an effective remedy for lavellan poisoning. Boiling the creature's head will also provide an antidote.

Each-uisge

Remote loch at night —
grisly neighs blend with downpour
blackening the hills

Commentary

In Scottish folklore, *each-uisge* ("water horse" in Scottish Gaelic) is a supernatural water horse reportedly found in the Scottish Highlands. Often confused for the *kelpie* (which inhabits streams and rivers), the *each-uisge* haunts the sea, sea lochs, and freshwater lochs. Every loch in Scotland has its own *each-uisge*. The creature has shape-shifting abilities, disguising itself as a magnificent and sleek horse, a handsome man, or a giant bird. Those who mount the beast in its equine form are only safe for as long as the *each-uisge* is ridden in the interior of the land. However, the slightest glimpse or smell of water foreshadows the death of the rider, for the skin of the *each-usige* becomes sticky, and the creature instantly dives into the deepest part of the loch with its victim. After the unlucky person has drowned, the *each-uisge* tears them apart and devours the entire body except for the liver, which floats onto the surface.

Traditionally, people in the Highlands were often wary of lone animals and strangers seen by the water's edge, near where an *each-uisge* was rumoured to live.

Murder Most Foul

Lonesome carnyx blows —
cold waves splash over the corpse
wreathed in pools of blood

Commentary

The haiku poem above, set in ancient Scotland, was inspired by one of the first scenes in David Lynch's *Twin Peaks*. In the sequence, Laura Palmer's dead body is found on the desolate shore of a lake. Prior to the horrific discovery, one of the main characters says: *lonesome foghorn blows*.

Carnyces (sing. *carnyx*) were large trumpets, usually made of bronze and brass and shaped like the head of an animal. They were widely utilised in the Iron Age Celtic world, mainly for military and ritual purposes. Due to the thunderous and harsh sounds they made, *carnyces* were used to raise the army's morale and to intimidate enemies.

Aonaranachd

On this stygian heath
the hearth in the remote broch
is cold and moistened

Commentary

A broch is a type of circular tower from the Iron Age with hollow, double-layered walls. The distribution of brochs is centred on Orkney and Shetland and parts of the Scottish mainland. These monumental structures formed a strong visual presence in the landscape of the Highlands and Islands, where many of them still survive almost to their original height. It has been estimated that the main period of the use of brochs was from the 2nd century BCE to the 2nd century CE, though radiocarbon dating suggests that the construction of the first brochs may have begun as early as 400 BCE.[33]

The haiku poem above depicts an abandoned broch located in a remote glen in the Scottish Highlands. The title of the poem is in Scottish Gaelic and it translates as "loneliness" or "solitude". The word *stygian* means "extremely dark, gloomy, or forbidding".

---

[33]   B. Cunliffe, *Iron Age Communities in Britain*, p. 335.

Pibroch I

An inclement dawn —
keening crones break down in tears
as soft pipes play on

Pibroch II

Through rain, sleet, and mist
by hollows, hirsts, and hillocks
rough rustlers roamed on

Pibroch III

Loud the wind wails
yet the wee boat smoothly sails
on these rogue sea waves

Commentary

A pibroch is a form of music for the Scottish bagpipes, which involves a series of variations on a basic theme, typically of a martial or funerary character. Music of a similar nature, preceding the adoption of the Highland pipes, may have been played on the wire-strung Gaelic harp (*clàrsach*). There are four major thematic categories of pibroch: mournful laments (*Cumha*), salutes commemorating important events (*Fàilte*), rallying tunes (*Port Tionail*), and rowing songs.

The first poem above depicts a funeral happening somewhere in the Scottish Highlands. Additional inspiration was derived from μ-Ziq's track *Soft Pipes Play On*. The second poem was inspired by the rallying pibroch of the Clan MacFarlane, which occupied the western side of Loch Lomond. The third poem was inspired by the lyrics of the *Skye Boat Song*, a famous late 19th-century song recalling the journey of Prince Charles Edward Stuart from Benbecula to the Isle of Skye.

Éiteag

A horrid hag howls —
white rapids at the loch's mouth
turn the rover's boat

Commentary

In Scottish folklore, *Éiteag* (meaning "the little foul or horrid one") is a malevolent spirit said to inhabit Loch Etive in Argyll. The meaning of her name probably alludes to the stormy and unpredictable weather that makes the rapids at the entrance of the lake (The Falls of Lora) particularly dangerous. The haiku poem above depicts how *Éiteag* causes a lone rover's boat to be overturned by the rapids.

Hebridean Mermaid

While men cut the kelp
a stream of euphonious sounds
comes from the stark dunes

Commentary

In 1830, a group of men were busy cutting kelp (a type of seaweed) at Sgeir na Duchadh on Benbecula, an island in the Outer Hebrides off the west coast of Scotland. Suddenly, one woman spotted an odd, mermaid-like creature. The workers were alarmed, and they waded into the water in an attempt to catch the mermaid. Though she evaded them, a boy threw a rock at the back of her head. Injured, the creature cried out in pain and disappeared beneath the waves. A few days later, the mermaid's lifeless body washed upon the shore a few kilometres north of where she had been spotted. According to local eyewitnesses, she resembled in shape a well-developed woman, though in size she looked like a little child. Her skin was pale, and the creature had long, dark, glossy hair. It is believed that the mermaid is buried either in the local churchyard or beneath the dunes.

Gamhnach

Thrown to the water
a wisp of fresh-cut green grass
makes the pow milk-white

Commentary

Gamhnach is the name of a small stream on Benbecula, an island in the Outer Hebrides off the west coast of Scotland. The name of the brook means "the farrow cow". According to W. J. Watson, it was customary to throw a wisp of green grass into Gamhnach as it was crossed, with the formula *fodar do'n Ghamhnaich*, meaning "fodder for the Gamhnach". As the evidence suggests, Gamhnach might have been a tutelary spirit from Benbecula, whose role was to protect the cattle.[34]

The dialectal word *pow* means "a creek or slow stream".

---

34   W. J. Watson, *The Celtic Place-names of Scotland*, p. 427.

The Broch of Gurness

The smell of fine wine
lingers in the chieftain's hold;
late November glee

Commentary

A broch is a type of circular tower from the Iron Age with hollow, double-layered walls. The distribution of brochs is centred on Orkney and Shetland and parts of the Scottish mainland. These monumental structures formed a strong visual presence in the landscape of the Highlands and Islands, where many of them still survive almost to their original height. It has been estimated that the main period of the use of brochs was from the 2nd century BCE to the 2nd century CE, though radiocarbon dating suggests that the construction of the first brochs may have begun as early as 400 BCE.[35]

During the Roman invasion of Britain, the "King of Orkney" was one of eleven British leaders who submitted to Emperor Claudius in 43 CE at Colchester. At the broch of Gurness, on the north-east coast of Mainland Orkney, archaeologists have found shards of a small amphora dating to before 60 CE. They were used to transport wine, which may have been a diplomatic gift from Rome.[36] The Broch of Gurness was probably home to the chief family of the community. With its thick walls, it may also have been a defensive site. It is unknown when the tower was constructed, though a period between 200 BCE and 100 BCE has been suggested. At some point after 100 CE, the broch of Gurness was deserted. In the Pictish period, some of its stones were reused to build smaller dwellings on top of the earlier buildings.

---

35   B. Cunliffe, *Iron Age Communities in Britain*, p. 335.

36   A. Moffat, *The Faded Map: Lost Kingdoms of Scotland*, p. 26.

Drustan's Wistfulness

Distant snow-capped peaks
loom out of the mirkning's mists;
bells toll in faint breeze

Commentary

The haiku poem above, set in the late 8th century, depicts a chilly evening somewhere in mainland Ross-shire, in the Scottish Highlands. The poem conveys a sense of autumnal wistfulness experienced by an elderly Pictish chieftain called Drustan. He spreads his gaze over the distant Munroes, barely visible in the growing dusk.[37] The tolling of the church bells contrasts with the wildness of the landscape, reminding Drustan of his grandfather Bridei who was a secret worshipper of old heathen deities. Although it appears that the elites of the entire Pictland had been formally Christianised by the early 7th century, the vestiges of pagan religion might have lingered among the general population for another century.

The Scottish dialectal word (nowadays used only in Orkney) *mirkning* is probably a borrowing from Old Norse, and it means "late twilight", "dusk".

---

37   Munro is defined as a peak in Scotland with a height over 3,000 feet (914.4 m).

Cù-sìth

Loose shreds of green fur
haunt the malodorous lair
where no man could fare

Three blood-curdling yowls —
the blaring sound of church bells
through the dreich moorland

Commentary

In Scottish folklore, the *Cù-sìth* is a large mythological hound said to roam the Scottish Highlands. The best inspired particular horror in the Hebrides, where it was thought to dwell in the clefts of rocks. The *Cù-sìth* is usually depicted as having a furry, dark green coat and being as big as a calf. Though the creature was capable of hunting noiselessly, it would occasionally let out three bone-chilling barks that could be heard for miles, even far out at sea. According to legend, those who hear the howling of the *Cù-Sìth* must reach safety by the third bark; otherwise, they are overwhelmed with panic to the point of not being able to move.

The first poem above describes the lair of the *Cù-sìth*. According to *Superstitions of the Highlands and Islands of Scotland*, the beast was said to inhabit a natural recess in the rocks of the shore at Baluaig on the Isle of Tiree. The location was known to locals as the Bed of the Fairy Dog.[38] The second poem above depicts the hound's barks heard across a Hebridean moorland. In a local church, the bells are rung to counteract the wickedness of the beast and to prevent it from approaching human settlements.

---

38   J. Campbell, *Superstitions of the Highlands and Islands of Scotland*, 1900.

Cait

Hosts of moaning gale
blow fiercely across the moors;
faint light in the broch

Commentary

Cait or Cat was a Pictish kingdom centred in what is now Caithness in northern Scotland. From an etymological perspective, the name *Cait* refers to the totemic name of a local tribe that probably held wild cats in sacred reverence. Similarly, the name of the Orkney Islands contains the tribal toponym *orc-*, which is usually interpreted as "young pig" or "young boar". According to a later medieval legend, the kingdom was founded by Caitt (or Cat), one of the seven sons of the ancestral figure Cruithne. The territory of Cait comprised not only modern Caithness, but also south-eastern Sutherland.

A broch is a type of circular tower from the Iron Age with hollow, double-layered walls. The distribution of brochs is centred on Orkney and Shetland and parts of the Scottish mainland. These monumental structures formed a strong visual presence in the landscape of the Highlands and Islands, where many of them still survive almost to their original height. It has been estimated that the main period of the use of brochs was from the 2nd century BCE to the 2nd century CE, though radiocarbon dating suggests that the construction of the first brochs may have begun as early as 400 BCE.[39]

The haiku poem above, set sometime around 100 BCE, depicts a stormy October night in the land of Cait. Only the dim light in the promontory broch of Crosskirk stands out from the dreich moorland. Radiocarbon chronology dates the construction of the broch to around 200 BCE. The

---

39   B. Cunliffe, *Iron Age Communities in Britain*, p. 335.

round tower was built within an older promontory fortification with a ring wall and blockhouse. The site was still in use in the 2nd century CE. It included a guard cell, an intramural chamber, and a stair entrance at ground level. The tower was surrounded by buildings that are believed to have been a village, an arrangement found only in northern Scotland. These dwellings were occupied from about the same time as the broch was constructed.

Erc Mocudruidi

Cold shafts of moonlight
shine on the seal-skinned robber;
glint of the murga

Commentary

In the 7th-century *Life of Saint Columba* (attributed to Adamnán of Iona), Erc Mocudruidi (whose name means "Erc, Son of the Druid") was a wretched robber who dwelt on the island of Colonsay in the Inner Hebrides off the west coast of Scotland. During the day, Erc was said to hide among the dunes, under his boat which he covered with hay. At night, the ruffian was in the habit of sailing to the nearby island and stealthily killing young seals, which were the property of Columba's monastery at Iona.

Columba ordered two monks to bring Erc to him. They captured the thief, whom they escorted back to Iona. Columba gave the ruffian a stern reprimand. As an expression of his goodwill, however, the saint offered some freshly killed sheep as compensation for the seals Erc would otherwise have stolen. In the epilogue to the story, Columba experienced a vision in which he sensed that Erc was close to death. The saint immediately ordered another monk to take a gift of sheep meat and six pecks of corn to the dying man. Unfortunately, Erc had died suddenly the same day, and the gifts sent over were consumed at his funeral feast.

Archaeologists have found that seal meat was consumed by the monks from Iona. Skin and oil from these animals were also valuable products. The sporrans worn with Scottish kilts are traditionally made from sealskin, though nowadays artificial materials are more common. In Columba's time, Irish seal-hunters used a special harpoon called a *murga* ("sea spear") or *rongai* ("seal spear"). Adult grey seals are large predators and can severely injure any human whom they perceive as a threat. The lone robber would have been well aware of this danger. Therefore, he did not attempt to slaughter full-grown male seals. Instead, his target was the breeding-ground of seals where mothers and newborns would have been particularly vulnerable to attacks. British and Irish grey seals breed in autumn, so Erc's nightly hunting trips probably took place in October or November.

The haiku poem above depicts Erc preparing for his nocturnal thievery.

Immram

The azure lagoon —
a boat sails out to the sea
speckled with sunspots

Commentary

Coastal lagoons are areas of shallow, coastal salt water, fully or partially separated from the sea by sandbanks, shingle or, less frequently, rocks. In Scotland, there are over one hundred saline lagoons. They are located mainly on the low-lying coastlines of the Western Isles and the northern archipelagos of Orkney and Shetland, though scattered examples dot the mainland's coast.

An *immram* (plural *immrama*) is an Old Irish literary genre of epic tales, which focus on a hero's sea journey to the Otherworld. Typically, the protagonist sets out on his marine voyage for the sake of thrill and adventure or to fulfil his destiny, and usually stops on other magical islands before reaching his final destination. In these stories, not all those who embark on *immrama* are able to return home. According to some scholars, the *immrama* may be distorted retellings of historical sea travels. There is no doubt that marine voyages of the early Irish monks were distant. They reached Orkney, Shetland, and the Faroe Islands at an early date and perhaps even travelled to Iceland.

The boat depicted in the poem above is a *curragh*, a type of a small vessel indigenous to Ireland. Traditionally, it was constructed of a wicker-work frame, covered with hides and stitched together with thongs. Some *curraghs* had a double hide-covering, some triple. These vessels are mentioned continuously in both lay and ecclesiastical literature. Depending on the weather and other circumstances, they were propelled by either oars or sails. Many *curraghs* were so small and light as to be easily carried on a man's back. When designed for long voyages, *curraghs* were made large and durable. They were furnished with masts, as well as solid decks and seats. The method of constructing *curraghs* has been described by foreign as well as by Irish writers. *The Voyage of Saint Brendan the Abbot* depicts how St. Brendan and his companions built a boat, in preparation for their voyage on the Atlantic:

"Using iron tools, they prepared a very light vessel, with wicker-work sides and ribs, after the manner of that country, and covered it with cowhide, tanned in oak-bark, tarring its joints: and they put on board provisions for forty days, with butter enough to dress hides for covering the boat [whenever the covering needed repair], and all utensils necessary for the use of the crew."[40]

The haiku poem above describes a 7th-century monk living in the Hebrides embarking on a short marine journey in his *curragh*.

---

40   P. W. Joyce, *A Smaller Social History of Ancient Ireland*, 1906.

Ogham: Gort

In forsaken fort
vine scales the lichen-grey walls;
russet oak leaves sigh

Commentary

Ogham writing is an early medieval alphabetic script dating from the 4th century CE, used primarily for writing the Irish and Pictish languages on stone monuments. According to early Irish sagas and legends, it was also utilised for writing messages on pieces of wood or metal, though there is no material evidence to support this. In its most common form, Ogham consists of four sets of strokes, or notches; each group comprised five letters composed of one to five strokes, thus giving twenty letters. These were carved along the edge of a stone, often vertically or from right to left.

The origin of Ogham is not clear. Some scholars point to a possible connection with the runic alphabets, while others claim that Ogham is merely a transformation of the Latin alphabet. Legendary accounts attribute the creation of Ogham script to Ogma (or Ogmios), the god of poetry and eloquence. The inscriptions in Ogham are concise, usually consisting of a personal name and patronymic in the genitive case. The majority of Ogham inscriptions is scattered through Ireland and Wales, though a few isolated specimens are also found in Cornwall, Devon, Scotland, and the Isle of Man. In early Irish literature, the names of individual Ogham letters were explained by lists of kennings known as *Bríatharogam*.

Gort is the twelfth letter of the Ogham alphabet. Folk tradition connects Gort with the ivy-plant.

The haiku poem above, set in the 6th century, depicts an abandoned

Roman fort on Hadrian's Wall. A fierce storm uprooted a massive oak, which fell over and landed on the crumbling wall. Now, the ivy is scaling the battlements and accelerating the process of their complete dilapidation. The haiku was inspired by an anonymous Anglo-Saxon poem called *The Ruin*, which evokes the former glory of a ruined Roman city.

Ogham: Ngéadal

Moors in yellow glow —
feral ponies nibble gorse
on this cloudy noon

Commentary

Ogham writing is an early medieval alphabetic script dating from the 4th century CE, used primarily for writing the Irish and Pictish languages on stone monuments. According to early Irish sagas and legends, it was also utilised for writing messages on pieces of wood or metal, though there is no material evidence to support this. In its most common form, Ogham consists of four sets of strokes, or notches; each group comprised five letters composed of one to five strokes, thus giving twenty letters. These were carved along the edge of a stone, often vertically or from right to left.

The origin of Ogham is not clear. Some scholars point to a possible connection with the runic alphabets, while others claim that Ogham is merely a transformation of the Latin alphabet. Legendary accounts attribute the creation of Ogham script to Ogma (or Ogmios), the god of poetry and eloquence. The inscriptions in Ogham are concise, usually consisting of a personal name and patronymic in the genitive case. The majority of Ogham inscriptions is scattered through Ireland and Wales, though a few isolated specimens are also found in Cornwall, Devon, Scotland, and the Isle of Man. In early Irish literature, the names of individual Ogham letters were explained by lists of kennings known as *Bríatharogam*.

Ngéadal is the thirteenth letter of the Ogham alphabet. Folk tradition connects *Ngéadal* with reed, or, according to alternative interpretation, gorse (*Ulex europaeus*).

The haiku poem above, set in contemporary Scotland, depicts Exmoor ponies nibbling shrubs of gorse below Traprain Law in East Lothian. Pale autumn sunlight is shining on these plants, enhancing their yellow hue. Traprain Law is an Iron Age *oppidum* (hillfort), believed to be one of the major settlements of the Votadini people. In 1919, archaeologists discovered a large hoard of silver from the Roman era at the site. A few centuries later, Traprain Law was one of the strongholds of the kingdom of Gododdin, the descendants of the Votadini. Today, visitors to the hill can see small herds of Exmoor ponies — a rare breed of semi-feral horses.

Ogham: Straif

Thonged blackthorn cudgel
breaks the ruffian's rough hand;
shelved sloe gin stays safe

Commentary

Ogham writing is an early medieval alphabetic script dating from the 4th century CE, used primarily for writing the Irish and Pictish languages on stone monuments. According to early Irish sagas and legends, it was also utilised for writing messages on pieces of wood or metal, though there is no material evidence to support this. In its most common form, Ogham consists of four sets of strokes, or notches; each group comprised five letters composed of one to five strokes, thus giving twenty letters. These were carved along the edge of a stone, often vertically or from right to left.

The origin of Ogham is not clear. Some scholars point to a possible connection with the runic alphabets, while others claim that Ogham is merely a transformation of the Latin alphabet. Legendary accounts attribute the creation of Ogham script to Ogma (or Ogmios), the god of poetry and eloquence. The inscriptions in Ogham are concise, usually consisting of a personal name and patronymic in the genitive case. The majority of Ogham inscriptions is scattered through Ireland and Wales, though a few isolated specimens are also found in Cornwall, Devon, Scotland, and the Isle of Man. In early Irish literature, the names of individual Ogham letters were explained by lists of kennings known as *Bríatharogam*.

Straif is the fourteenth letter of the Ogham alphabet. Folk tradition connects *straif* with blackthorn trees.

The haiku poem above, set in early modern Ireland, depicts a mischievous drunkard who breaks into a household in an attempt to steal a bottle of sloe gin. He is, however, stopped by an elderly man who crushes his hand with a sturdy blackthorn cudgel. In Ireland, blackthorn wood is used to make a *shillelagh*, which is a traditional walking stick or cudgel with a large knob at the top. These clubs are widely utilised in *bataireacht*, a form of Irish stick-fighting martial arts. In Britain and Ireland, sloe gin is a red liqueur drink made from ripe blackthorn fruit (sloes), which are usually picked after the first frost (from late October to early November). Each sloe is pricked with a thorn taken from the blackthorn bush on which they grow.

Ogham: Ruis

Thick elder hedgerow —
warbling blackcaps rouse the maid
whose cheeks flush like flames

Commentary

Ogham writing is an early medieval alphabetic script dating from the 4th century CE, used primarily for writing the Irish and Pictish languages on stone monuments. According to early Irish sagas and legends, it was also utilised for writing messages on pieces of wood or metal, though there is no material evidence to support this. In its most common form, Ogham consists of four sets of strokes, or notches; each group comprised five letters composed of one to five strokes, thus giving twenty letters. These were carved along the edge of a stone, often vertically or from right to left.

The origin of Ogham is not clear. Some scholars point to a possible connection with the runic alphabets, while others claim that Ogham is merely a transformation of the Latin alphabet. Legendary accounts attribute the creation of Ogham script to Ogma (or Ogmios), the god of poetry and eloquence. The inscriptions in Ogham are concise, usually consisting of a personal name and patronymic in the genitive case. The majority of Ogham inscriptions is scattered through Ireland and Wales, though a few isolated specimens are also found in Cornwall, Devon, Scotland, and the Isle of Man. In early Irish literature, the names of individual Ogham letters were explained by lists of kennings known as Bríatharogam.

Ruis is the fifteenth letter of the Ogham alphabet. It is derived from *ruise*, meaning "red" or "reddening". Early medieval kennings refer to the reddening of the face caused by intense emotion (either anger or embarrassment), and other sources also mention the practice of reddening the cheeks with the juice of plants. Folk tradition connects *ruis* with elder trees.

The haiku poem above depicts a hedgerow made of elder trees somewhere in southern Scotland. Eurasian blackcaps feed on elderberries, and their melodic songs rouse a maid who was sleeping in the thicket. It is not clear what caused the woman's cheeks to flush, perhaps she had slept there with her secret lover who abandoned her at dawn.

PART SEVEN

IRELAND

Geniti-glinni

Echoing wild screams —
the smokefall's abysmal brume
obscures hosts of sprites

Commentary

In Irish mythology, the *Geniti-glinni* (meaning "the sprites of the valley") were malevolent and fierce apparitions who delighted in carnage. These female sprites were said to inhabit isolated, lonely glens (deep, narrow valleys). They were sometimes accompanied by the *Demna aeir*, "demons of the air". When there was a fight, the *Geniti-glinni* were heard shrieking and howling with delight, some amid the fray, others far off in their solitary retreats.

The story of *The Feast of Bricriu* tells how the three great Red Branch champions, Lóegaire the Victorious, Conall Cernach, and Cúchulainn contested one time for the *Curathmir*, or "champion's bit", which was always awarded to the most courageous and strongest hero. To determine this matter, the warriors were subjected to various feats and tests. At some point, it was decided that the three heroes were to separately attack a colony the *Geniti-glinni* that had their habitat in a nearby glen. Lóegaire went first; but the sprites instantly beset him with such fiendish savagery that he was glad to escape, half-naked, leaving them his arms and armour. Conall Cernach went next, and he fared somewhat better, for, though leaving his spear on the battlefield, he managed to keep his sword.

Finally, Cúchulainn went. The imps filled his ears with piercing howls, and assailing him, they shattered his shield and spear and tore his garments to tatters. At last, he could bear it no longer and exhibited apparent signs of fleeing. However, his loyal charioteer, Láeg, was observing the fight closely. One of Láeg's duties was to shower reproaches on his master, whenever he saw him about to lose a battle. The charioteer berated Cúchulainn so vehemently and bitterly for his weakness, and poured out such disdainful nicknames on him, that the champion became enraged. Having regained courage and the will to fight, Cúchulainn turned on the devilish war-furies once more, and, sword in hand, he crushed and hacked them to pieces. Afterwards, the glen was all red with their blood.[41]

The haiku poem above depicts a colony of the *Geniti-glinni*. The word *smokefall* is usually defined as "misty dusk", and *brume* is an archaic word for late autumn or winter fog.

---

41   P. W. Joyce, *A Smaller Social History of Ancient Ireland*, 1906.

Anamchara

Whispers in the cell —
still lake in tawny colours
of this brisk twilight

Commentary

The phrase *anamchara* refers to the early Irish concept of the soul friend in religious matters. In medieval Irish monasticism, it applied to a monk's teacher, confessor, companion, or spiritual guide. According to Nora Chadwick, the term *anamchara* originally referred to a fellow monk sharing one's cell, to whom an individual confessed, revealing confidential aspects of their life.[42]

The setting of the poem is Gougane Barra, a serene glacial valley located in County Cork, Ireland. The valley is most famous for its small church, built in the 19th century on an island in the lake called Loch Irce. The temple was erected near the ruins of a 6th-century monastic site, founded by Saint Finbarr of Cork. The haiku depicts a peaceful autumn afternoon on the lake, sometime in the early medieval period. Whispers in the cell refer to an act of confession taking place in the quietude of the nearby oratory. A monk confesses his sins to another anchorite, his trusted *anamchara*. The poem attempts to convey a sense of communion between nature and man, characteristic of early medieval monasticism.

---

42 N. Chadwick, *The Age of the Saints in the Early Celtic Church* (London: Oxford University Press, 1963).

An Drochshaol

A failure of bread —
dark sun over gloomy fields
where scrawny cows graze

Commentary

The Great Irish Famine (also known in Irish as *An Drochshaol*, "hard times") was a famine that affected Ireland in 1845–49 when the potato harvest failed in successive years. The crop failures were caused by late blight, a disease that damages both the leaves and the edible roots of the potato plant.

The haiku poem above does not, however, refer to the Great Irish Famine in the 19th century. Both the *Annals of Ulster* and the *Annals of Inisfallen* recorded "a failure of bread in the year 536". The event is thought to have been the result of a severe and sudden cooling of the climate, which in turn could have been caused by a massive volcanic eruption around that time. Its effects were widespread, causing anomalies of colder weather, crop failures, and famines worldwide.

Sírecht

Secluded homestead —
the widower lies restless
while cold stars twinkle

Commentary

Sírecht is an Irish word referring to a feeling of nostalgia, wistfulness, and homesickness, similar to the untranslatable Welsh word *hiraeth*. It also describes a yearning for home that one cannot return to, no longer exists, or maybe never was.

The haiku poem above depicts a 7th-century Irish homesteader (*bóaire*) who lost his wife to the so-called Yellow Plague of 664. According to the *Annals of Tigernach*, the plague was preceded by a solar eclipse: "darkness on the 1st of May, at the ninth hour and in the same summer the sky seemed to be on fire". Bede the Venerable mentions that the disease "depopulated first the southern parts of Britain", and then spread to Northern Britain and Ireland. The Annals of Ulster add that "the plague reached Ireland on the 1st of August". Its impact was immediate and devastating, in the south-east initially but soon spreading to the rest of the country.

In Vedic astrology, Rahu and Ketu are Sanskrit names given to the Nodes of the Moon: the North Node and South Node, respectively. They are not physical bodies, but two points (that are 180 degrees apart) at which the Moon's orbit intersects the ecliptic, the apparent path of the Sun around the Earth. When the Moon crosses the ecliptic, it disturbs the electromagnetic field and this can create eclipses, which are considered full of occult significance. Eclipses represent the unfolding of powerful karmic energies, and they may foreshadow collective catastrophes such as earthquakes and plagues.[43]

In early medieval Irish society, *bóaire* was a title meaning "the cow lord", given to an owner of a farmstead or business. A *bóaire* was a wealthy free-man with loyalties to a clan chief. Some historians argue that it was the first rank of nobility (*aire*). However, legal tracts from this period explicitly state that members of this class were ranked below the noble grades, though above the unfree.

---

43   K. Sutton, *The Lunar Nodes: Crisis and Redemption* (Bournemouth: The Wessex Astrologer, 2001), p. 1.

Murchoirthe

Abandoned clocháns —
bitter is the wind tonight
on this lonesome isle

Commentary

In early medieval Ireland, *murchoirthe* was a legal term designating a category of outsiders. The word *murchoirthe* translates as "one thrown up by the sea, a castaway". In some cases, it referred to a criminal set adrift on the sea as a punishment. The word in question was also connected to *muirchrech*, another legal term, which denoted a particular distance on the sea.[44]

The haiku poem above, set in the 9th century, depicts an outcast marooned on Inishmurray (*Inis Muireadheach*), a then-uninhabited island located off the coast of what is now County Sligo.

It is said that Saint Molaise founded a monastery on Inishmurray in the 6th century. The site contained various ecclesiastical structures including enclosures, a stone-roofed oratory, two churches, *clocháns* (beehive-shaped huts made of dry-stone), a holy well, and other remains including cross-slabs, suggesting foreign influences. The whole complex was built of what is probably local sandstone rubble. The island's ecclesiastical settlement was attacked in 795 and again in 807 by the Vikings. Eventually, the monks abandoned the island and it remained uninhabited until its first secular settlement, probably in the 12th century.

The second line of the haiku was inspired by an anonymous early medieval Irish poem:

---

44   For more information about sea-boundaries in early medieval Ireland, please refer to the following paper: P. O'Neill, *Old Irish Muirchrech 'Sea-Boundary'*, Ériu, vol. 67, 2017, pp. 1–9.

Bitter is the wind tonight
It tosses the ocean's white hair
Tonight I fear not the fierce warriors of Norway
Coursing on the Irish sea

This short poem conveys a sense of dread inherent to life in Irish ecclesiastical communities in the 9th century, when Viking raids on monasteries were an ever-present danger.

Cluan Innis

Patches of blue sky
in the bog's murky water
circling the tower

Commentary

Cluan Innis is the Old Irish name for Clones, a small town in western County Monaghan, Ireland. It is said that Clones was surrounded by marshes, hence its name *Cluan Innis* meaning "island of retreat". In 1606, the English poet Sir John Davies wrote that roads from Clones "were nigh impassable due to bogs".

Clones was the site of a monastic settlement founded by Saint Tighearnach in the 6th century. The ruins of a 12th-century abbey building can still be found in the town, along with a sarcophagus thought to have been built to store the remains of Saint Tighearnach. Next to the ruins is a round tower and a high cross.

The round tower, depicted in the haiku above, would have originally stood at almost twenty-three metres in height, including the conical cap which is now missing. The cap was lost between 1591 and 1741, and the base shows evidence of attempts to destroy by burning. The building was erected from sandstone around the 10th century. It originally had five floors accessible by ladders. The purpose of round towers is not clear, though it has been suggested that besides serving the function of belfries, they may have been store-houses or places of refuge in the case of sudden Viking raids.

Cnoc Gréine

Autumn is coming —
high votive flames burn fiercely
as nights grow colder

Commentary

Cnoc Gréine ("hill of Grian") is a prominent hill in eastern County Limerick near Pallas Grean, Ireland. The site is thought to be a *sídh* (a hill or mound in which fairies, gods, or ancestral spirits live) of Grian, a local pre-Christian divinity. Grian may have been a solar deity, since her name stems from the Proto-Indo-European root **gwher-*, meaning "to be hot" or "to burn". She is occasionally considered synonymous with Macha, a sovereignty goddess of ancient Ireland.

According to a local legend, when the five sons of the Irish hero Conall tried to attack the fairy mound of Cnoc Gréine, the goddess Grian turned them into badgers. Perhaps these five champions were transformed into badgers because they sought the secrets they were not entitled to as men, but which were suitable for badgers, the keepers of underground lore. These nocturnal mammals are equipped with short legs and sharp claws by nature, which are ideal for digging. Badgers create extensive underground dwellings called setts, with tunnels connecting chambers that are lined with dry bedding material such as grass, moss, and bracken.

The haiku poem above depicts a large bonfire lit on *Cnoc Gréine* on the occasion of a harvest festival, the holiday connected with the Autumn equinox.

Fianna

Wooded mountain pass —
flaring heads of their great spears
flush in afterglow

Díberga

Ambushed in thick fog
travelling nuns cry for help
as wolf-heads seize them

Commentary

In ancient Indo-European societies, unmarried young men often joined small semi-independent groups living on the fringes of society. These warrior brotherhoods, organised around the person of a powerful leader, engaged in cattle raiding, pillaging hostile settlements, and hunting. Such groups facilitated a young man's transition from childhood into adulthood. They provided him with an opportunity to prove his manhood, courage, and skills before he was accepted as an adult member of his tribe. Similar rites of passage have existed for millennia in practically every tradition on earth. In ancient Germanic societies, such war-bands are usually referred to as *Männerbünde*. In ancient Ireland, they were known as the *Fianna*.

A *fiann* consisted of landless young men, frequently young aristocrats who had not yet come into their inheritance of land. A member of a *fiann* was called a *fénnid*; the leader of a *fiann* was known as a *rígfénnid*. They attained their greatest power during the reign of Cormac mac Art (mid-3rd century CE) under their most renowned *rígfénnid* Finn. The first poem above depicts a *fiann* wandering through the wooded hills of Connacht.

In the second poem, nuns travelling from one monastery to another are ambushed by marauding brigands, who belong to a different, more sinister kind of warrior brotherhood. The terms *díberg* and *láech* in Irish, and *laicus* or *latronus* in Latin, designated a member of a band of highwaymen who sought to cause social disorder, either by killing sprees or by raiding churches. Early Irish penitentials single them out as being unable to receive a pardoning of their sins through expiation.[45]

Díberga are recognised in Irish literature by their distinct insignia, described as *signa diabolica* or *stigmata*. In the *Latin Life of Lugaid*, a devilish band (*scola diaboli*) approached the saint and his community. The brigands were wearing *vexilla* on their heads. In Latin, *vexillum* typically refers to a standard or a flag. This text, however, suggests that this was some form of headgear. It could be seen from afar and was recognisable for what it was, as Lugaid caught sight of the brigands and, blessing his community, ordered them to seek shelter in the woods. *The Life of Brigit*, attributed to Cogitosus, provides a clear routine of their ritualistic principles of conduct:

"Brigit saw nine men in a peculiar guise required by a godless and diabolical superstition, shouting in a grotesque tone of voice and showing signs of utter insanity, and in their paths lay destruction and misfortune. With their most wicked vows and oaths to the ancient enemy who reigned over them, they thirsted for bloodshed and planned the slaughter and murder of others before the calends of the following months should arrive."

This code consisted of distinctive attire, intimidating and loud noise, frenzy, and violent activities at certain times of the year. Mutilation, killing, death, and finally rebirth form part of a universal code for initiation rites. *Díberga* were probably tattooed or scarred, renamed, and donned animal skins in the various steps towards their second birth. A trace of such practices may have survived in Irish personal names such as *Cennfaelad*, "wolfhead", *Faelan*, "little wolf", and *Faelgus* "wolf vigour".[46]

---

45   E. Bhreathnach, *Ireland in the Medieval World AD 400-100* (England: Four Courts Press, 2014), p. 141.

46   *Ibid.*, p. 142.

Fer coirthe

A sad stag bellows —
a vagrant's rest on damp moss
in the leafless copse

Commentary

In Old Irish, *fer coirthe* means "wanderer", "vagrant".[47] The haiku poem above was inspired by an early medieval Irish poem called *Scél lem dúib*, which has been given the English title "Summer has Gone". The haiku intends to convey a sense of loneliness experienced by the wandering man. Exiled from his tribe (*tuath*),[48] he is prevented from finding shelter among living people. Weary and overtaken by despondency (*domenma*), he decides to lay down on the moss in the woods and try to sleep until dawn. Sweet repose, however, does not come — for it is already late October and the woods are made inhospitable by cold wind and dampness. The atmosphere of desolation is additionally intensified by a mournful roar of a stag that rouses the vagrant from his half-conscious state between sleep and wakefulness.

---

47   D. Ó Cróinín, *Early Medieval Ireland 400-1200* (Harlow: Longman, 1995), p. 297.

48   For more information about the notion of exile and its connection with kingship in early Irish literature, please refer to the following paper:

       G. Bondarenko, *King in Exile in Airne Fíngein ('Fíngen's Vigil'): power and pursuit in Early Irish literature, Etudes Celtiques*, vol. 36, 2008. pp. 135-148.

Gormflaith

Blue blooms and blonde hair
dropped down the pellucid well;
where has the lass gone?

Commentary

Gormflaith is an Irish language female given name meaning "blue princess" or "distinguished princess". It is also a Gaelic mythological personification of Ireland. The word Gormflaith is a compound of the Irish words *gorm* ("blue") and *flaith* ("sovereign"). Irish texts note Gormflaith as the name of several queens closely associated with dynastic politics in early medieval Ireland. It was one of the most popular Gaelic female forenames between the 8th and 16th century.

Cath Mag Itha

Leaves brought by stiff wind
cloak these exposed, grassless knolls
where fallen kings sleep

Commentary

According to Irish mythology, Mag Itha was the site of the first battle fought in Ireland. Different medieval sources calculated that the battle had taken place in or between 2668 BCE and 2580 BCE. The opposing sides of the conflict were the Fomorians, commanded by Cichol Gricenchos, and the followers of Partholón.

According to the *Lebor Gabála Érenn*, the Fomorians had dwelt in Ireland for 200 years, subsisting by fishing and fowling, before the arrival of Partholón. The latter's people were the first in Ireland to introduce the art of farming, architecture, and brewing beer. The *Lebor Gabála* dates Partholón's landing in Ireland to 2590 BCE and claims that the Battle of Mag Itha took place ten years after that event, in circa 2580 BCE.

The plain of Mag Itha is thought to have been cleared by Partholón's hireling Ith. The conflict took place on the *slemna*, or "smooth lands", of that plain. Three hundred Fomorians took part in the battle, and Partholón emerged victorious over his foes. The earliest versions of the *Lebor Gabála* state that Cichol was slain and the Fomorians defeated. Later revisions, however, claim that the Fomorians were one-armed and one-eyed creatures, that the battle lasted a week, and there were no casualties as it was fought entirely by magic. *The Annals of the Four Masters*, on the other hand, date the battle to circa 2668 BCE. The scripture states that eight hundred Fomorians took part in it, all of whom were killed. In his work *Foras Feasa ar Éirinn*, Geoffrey Keating also mentions Cath Mag Itha but provides little detail and no date.

Three hundred years after Partholón's arrival in Ireland, his people were eradicated by a mysterious plague. The haiku poem above depicts burial mounds on the plain of Mag Itha. These knolls are said to house the remains of the champions who fell in the battle.

Badb

A gurgling black crow
sits on the two-faced idol;
gusts ruffling tall grass

Commentary

In Irish mythology, Badb is a goddess associated with war and death. She often appears to foreshadow imminent bloodshed or to engage in battles, where she creates chaos among warriors. Badb takes the form of a screeching raven or crow, striking fear into those who hear her. Sometimes she is also seen as an ugly hag or a "washer at the ford". It has been suggested that Badb is closely related to the Gaulish goddess Catubodua.

The haiku poem above depicts the bilateral stone statue on Boa Island, an island near the north shore of Lower Lough Erne in County Fermanagh, Northern Ireland. The name of the island is etymologically related to the goddess Badb. Two anthropomorphic carved stone statues, the Boa Island figure and the Lustymore Island figure, are now found together in the Caldragh graveyard on Boa Island. The cemetery dates from the early Irish Christian period. Both of the figures were severely damaged when they were first found. They have been set beside each other on unrelated pillars in the graveyard, which is the original location of the Boa figure. The larger of the figures is considered to be one of the most mysterious and unusual stone figures in Ireland. It is called a Janus-figure because it has two faces, resembling the two-headed Roman deity Janus. However, it is unlikely to be a representation of Janus. The reasons for creating these stone sculptures and the dates of their erection are not certain.

Crom Cruach

Early morning sun
strikes the wizened colossus
clad in milky fog

Commentary

Crom Cruach was an agricultural deity worshipped in pre-Christian Ireland.

According to the 12th-century *Book of Leinster*, Crom Cruach's cult image was a statue made of gold and silver. The idol was surrounded by twelve smaller stone or brass figures. The structure was located on *Magh Slécht* ("the plain of prostration") in County Cavan and the deity was allegedly appeased with the sacrifice of a first-born in exchange for an excellent harvest of grain and abundance of milk. Crom Cruach is represented as a wizened god, obscured by mists, and is said to have been revered since the time of Érimón. An early historic High King, Tigernmas, along with three-quarters of his army, is thought to have died while worshipping Crom on *Samhain*. Nevertheless, worship continued until St Patrick smashed the idol with a sledgehammer. Some have interpreted the figure of Crom Cruach as the sun circled by twelve signs of the zodiac, implying a function as a solar deity.

In my interpretation, however, Crom Cruach bears a striking resemblance to the Greek deity Cronus or his Roman counterpart, Saturn. Cronus's functions were associated with agriculture. According to Plutarch, Cronus was imprisoned by Zeus on a remote island located west of Britain:

"An isle, Ogygia, lies far out at sea, distant five days' sail from Britain as you sail westward; and three other islands equally distant from it and from one another lie out from it in the general direction of the summer sunset.

In one of these, according to the tale told by the natives, Cronus is confined by Zeus, and the antique Briareus, holding watch and ward over those islands and the sea that they call the Cronian main, has been settled close beside him (...) For Cronus himself sleeps confined in a deep cave of rock that shines like gold — the sleep that Zeus has contrived like a bond for him — and birds flying in over the summit of the rock bring ambrosia to him, and all the island is suffused with fragrance scattered from the rock as from a fountain; and those spirits mentioned before tend and serve Cronus, having been his comrades what time he ruled as king over gods and men."[49]

---

49   Plutarch, *De Faciae*, 26.

Cathair Conraoi

Cold rain wets his brat
as he rides up to the rath;
dark November days

Commentary

Ringforts were circular fortified settlements built in ancient and early medieval Ireland. They are known as *raths* when an earthen bank surrounds them with an external ditch, and as *cashels* or *cahers* when the enclosure is a wall made of dry stone, usually without a trench. It is estimated that there may be thirty to forty thousand of these circular fortresses scattered throughout Ireland. Very occasionally, parts of the dry-stone buildings can still be seen today, and traces of small timber buildings have been unearthed by excavation. The vast majority of ringforts must be thought of as defensive homesteads. The largest ones, however, must have fulfilled a communal purpose, perhaps as tribal capitals. Some probably had an industrial nature, being shelters for metalworkers or pottery-makers who worked under the patronage of a tribal king.[50]

The haiku poem above depicts a misty November afternoon in the ringfort of *Cathair Conraoi*. The *rath* is situated on the slopes of Caherconree Mountain, the second-highest peak in the Slieve Mish Mountains in the Dingle Peninsula in County Kerry, Ireland. In Irish mythology, the fort is thought to have been built by Cú Roí Mac Daire, the legendary evil wizard and King of West Munster. *Cathair Conraoi* is one of the oldest place names to be found in the traditional literature of Ireland. *The Triads of Ireland* classify it as one of the three oldest settlements on Irish soil.

In the late 1850s, an expedition of the South Munster Antiquarian

---

50   L. Alcock, *Arthur's Britain*, p. 255-256.

Society climbed up to the top of Caherconree Mountain to explore the ruins of *Cathair Conraoi*. One of these antiquarians wrote a short poem after seeing his companions wrapped in the mountain's fog:

"We went our way, for 'twere dishonour
If e'er it should be said that we
Scared by the legends of the valley
Saw not the towers of old Conri.

No sooner went we up the mountain
That all at once we lost our way;
The mists in clouds came curling round us,
And led our eyes and steps astray."

Samhainn

The psychic's study —
the glow of the carved turnip
lights up the cold sphere

Commentary

Samhainn (or *Samhain*) is one of the most important Gaelic festivals, denoting the separation between summer and winter. It is celebrated from October 31 to November 1. The eve of *Samhainn* was a liminal time in which boundaries between the mundane world and the Otherworld were more likely to be crossed. It was believed that magical events and supernatural beings were more likely to be encountered on *Samhainn*. It was also a time of merry-making and social gatherings. In Scotland, great bonfires (*Samhnag*) were lit, which were considered to have protective and cleansing powers, and there were rituals involving them. Root vegetables, such as turnips and rutabagas (swedes), were carved. Nowadays, however, pumpkin carving is more common. In Ireland, guisers wore masks and went from house to house, asking for treats and threatening the residents with mischief if their requests were not satisfied. The night was known as *Mischief Night* in many places, and pranks were played in rural areas throughout Ireland and the Americas. All the above beliefs and customs have played a role in the formation of the contemporary festival of Halloween.

The haiku poem above, set in contemporary Ireland sometime during the late 1990s, depicts a solitary psychic medium looking into a crystal ball on the eve of *Samhainn*. The clairvoyant takes advantage of this special time of year, hoping to connect with the Otherworld.

I would like to thank Anthony Huso for providing me with inspiration for this poem.

Daoine Sídhe

Strange August evenings —
cool waft from the hazy mounds
where warmth still lingers

Commentary

In Irish mythology, the *Daoine Sídhe* were a supernatural race of spirits and gods, who were said to live underground beneath ancient burial mounds, megalithic structures, and hills. It was believed that boundaries between the mundane world and the Otherworld were thinner at dawn and dusk. Thus, sightings of the *Daoine Sídhe* were more common at these liminal times of the day. They are generally described as stunningly beautiful, though they can also appear as hideous monsters.

The haiku poem above depicts a typical August evening somewhere in western Ireland. Though the sun has just set behind the horizon, its warmth can still be felt among the ancient dolmens situated on a grassy knoll. At the same time, thin mist rises from the nearby river and descends upon the burial site. A strange waft of cold air emanates from the megalithic boulders, which creates an eerie impression of supernatural presence.

The poem was inspired by H. P. Lovecraft's short story *The Tomb*.

Móin Alúine

Late autumn darkness —
impenetrable marshlands
swarm with eldritch wights

Commentary

The haiku poem above depicts the Bog of Allen (*Móin Alúine* in Irish), a large raised bog in the central part of Ireland, between the rivers Liffey and Shannon. Due to the unique preservation conditions within peat, many archaeological artefacts which do not normally survive the passage of time are preserved. These include wooden structures and objects. In many parts of the Bog of Allen, industrial milling has revealed archaeological remains such as trackways. These wooden structures, built through prehistory and into the medieval period, enabled people and animals to cross the extensive areas of peatland. The archaeological evidence from the Bog of Allen provides us with valuable insight into the economy and way of life of the societies that revolved around the Irish bogs.

In 2003, an ancient bog body was found near Croghan Hill, the remains of an extinct volcano rising from the Bog of Allen. Named after the place where it was found, the Old Croghan Man is believed to have died between 362 BCE and 175 BCE. Bog bodies are human corpses that have been naturally mummified in a peat bog. The vast majority of specimens, found mostly in north-western Europe, dates to the Iron Age. The state of preservation of the discoveries varies, and the bones usually dissolve. However, bog bodies often retain their skin, hair, and internal organs. The combination of highly acidic water, total exclusion of air, and low temperature preserves their skin, though severely tans it.

The haiku poem above depicts the Bog of Allen in November, sometime in the Iron Age. Many atmospheric ghost lights appear above the bog. They represent spirits of the dead who had been thrown into the swamp, much like the Old Croghan Man.

Celtica and Infinity (A)

Purple clouds at dusk —
vague shapes of crystalline isles
far out in the sea

Celtica and Infinity (B)

Slowly lapping waves
wash over his cold, frail feet;
the druid's egress

Celtica and Infinity (C)

Bodhráns and great pipes
resound through the misty shore;
the rising half-moon

Commentary

The haiku poems above were inspired by Alan Stivell's album *Beyond Words*. For the full experience, they should ideally be read with the corresponding songs playing in the background.

The poems depict a tranquil beach facing the Atlantic Ocean, somewhere in County Kerry, in the south-west of Ireland. It was my intention to convey a sense of marine infinity perceived by a druid standing at the shore. In the first poem, vague shapes of crystalline isles allude to *Tír na nÓg*, a supernatural realm of eternal youth, beauty, health, prosperity, and joy. According to Irish folklore, an island called *Hy-Brasil* was visible from the west coast of Ireland for only one day every seven years, being concealed by fog the rest of the time. The second poem depicts the elderly druid's passing — he slowly disappears into the mist that descends upon the shore. He is magically taken to *Tír na nÓg* to dwell with *Tuatha Dé Danann*, a mythical race of gods.

Following the druid's disappearance, an eerie sound of drums and pipes resounds through the foggy shore, which is now partially lit by the rising crescent moon.

A *bodhrán* is a type of shallow, hand-held drum used in traditional Irish music. *Bodhráns* were traditionally played by being struck with an animal bone, or in modern times, a piece of wood. Although its origins are unclear, it has been suggested that the instrument may derive from the skin trays used in Ireland for carrying peat. Alternatively, the *bodhrán* may be a successor of similar frame drums used in more ancient times.

The *great pipes* in the third poem refer to an ancient predecessor of the uilleann pipes. This type of bagpipes, unique to Ireland, is played with air provided to the bag by a bellows compressed between the player's elbow and waist. The uilleann pipes are almost always played sitting down.

PART EIGHT

MISCELLANEOUS POEMS

The fog is so thick
that the oldest churchgoer
misses the vespers

The squealing sirens
echo through the smoggy air;
lost, sunless highway

Rustling of the leaves —
shadows mask a hooded shape
stalking the young lass

Auburn leaves lay low
amid old marble statues;
the alley at dusk

The sound of chainsaws —
rosy radiance fades away
behind brumous peaks

As daylight recedes
eerie shadows slowly scale
the windy hillside

The scent of cut hay
lingers in the misty fields;
distant church bells chime

Harsh blustery wind
pushes the black clouds away;
an elder's weak smile

At the daylight's gate
her wistful blue eyes follow
the lone crane's egress

Faint flames of twilight
kindle this eldritch beech holt
where dead stillness hangs

A gentle drizzle
masks a solitary tear
flowing from her eyes

The departing train
leaves the crying miss behind;
pink rail touched by rain

The gas lamp's strong niff
lingers in the chilly air;
nightly dance of moths

A rotting oak leaf
falls into the damp basement
through the cracked window

The boarded-up door
in an abandoned cellar;
the stench of bad meat

Harsh wind from the heath
bursts open the locked loft door;
bright moonlight pours in

Carpet of moist leaves —
once again the boy forgot
to take off his boots

Shafts of lunar rays
sneak into the deep mineshaft
where the trapped cats meow

What a foul foetor! —
in this chimney so narrow
a lone thief's corpse sprawled

One drying raindrop
disturbed by a cat's wet paw;
a scurrying mouse squeaks

Light rain strokes her cheeks
as she rakes leaves on the lawn;
how sadly they sough

Gloomy one-way street —
a gang of hired thugs concealed
in clouds of vapour

The ajar church door —
blurred reflection of red dusk
glimpsed by priest's glazed eyes

Long before daybreak
sweet birdsong lulls her to sleep;
bleary eyes squeeze shut

Twilight is long gone —
buzzing moths die in high flames
that consume the byre

The taste of bone broth
on a long chilly evening;
woodcutter's red cheeks

Grey hills at daybreak —
she harvests luscious rose hips
though tears dew her dress

Moth-eaten sweaters —
not even autumnal chill
will make her wear them

Handcuffed leaf-peeper
has lost the binoculars
he spied nude fawns with

Wings of the windmill
cut his twilit face in half;
scarecrow in wheat fields

Black lodge in the woods
where sunlight never comes in;
rusty wind chimes ring

When full moon comes out
the stuffed owls in the toy store
are not what they seem

Pub veiled in dull smoke —
pitiful saxophone wails
through incessant rain

Choked cries at midnight —
a warped reflection of moon
in her sightless eyes

Trapped in the dry well
a cat yowls pitifully;
deserted village

Grandfather's last gaze —
eyes close with the silent sun
sinking to the sea

Latticed rhubarb pie
at the kitchen windowsill;
patches of pink clouds

Wet drops of blue ink
drip from the broken bottle
to a pool of blood

Swirling of the leaves
in the abbey's bleak courtyard
where only wind dwells

Grey scrawny horses
stand still in the pouring rain;
desolate homestead

Columns of grey clouds
patch azure holes in the sky;
dogs stir the puddle

Wind blows through her braids
as she cycles down the downs
where light still lingers

The lighthouse keeper
snoring by the candlelight;
loud knock at the door

Through the rose window
moon shines on a tattered dress;
dark, musty garret

In the dank cavern
an unknown prisoner's bones
glint in cold moonlight

The lingering smog
among the blocks of concrete;
the bird's muffled song

A dying pigeon
entangled in the barbed wire;
pale sun behind fumes

Departing wild geese
leave a sharp scent of bleakness
in the old birch copse

Forsaken valley —
one icy star shows the way
to spectral shadows

A full glass of wine
left on the lew veranda;
breeze in the far fells

Droning twilight rain
blasts upon the sombre roofs;
even cats have hid

The warmth of the sun
hides behind the distant copse;
sweet silence settles

Stiff nocturnal wind
blows dry leaves into the cave;
swarms of bats pour out

A small mouse shivers
in the desolate cloister;
rain drums on the roof

Abandoned warehouse —
moonlight shines on rusty cars
through these large skylights

Relentless downpour —
a cracked mug of hot chocolate
spilled over the rug

Dropped by the drunk bum
a blue key to the girl's box
falls down the storm drain

Odd sound of laughing
on the top of the staircase
silvered by moonlight

An ear in the grass
half-eaten by hungry ants;
ghost town at wee hours

First date at the lake —
cherry pie tastes so luscious
when he smooths my hair

Lunch at the diner —
maple syrup on some ham
makes the hag's tongue slam

Smell of damn fine joe —
as we flee from drenching rain
this bar feels like home

Where they venture now
empyrean bird hymns resound
through the lush woodlands

Hideous shapes lurk
in this fathomless darkness;
eerie, mist-choked woods

Prowler in the dark —
when the chilly draught blows in
a candle goes out

Rattling of the chains —
white decrepit spectre moans
with the hissing wind

A creaking window
in the dead sorcerer's spire;
gusty autumn night

A nightly downpour —
raindrops fall down the storm drain
where a rat's skull lies

Last day on the porch —
weak sunlight on the old man's
pale and haggard face

Two deafs cross the tracks —
headlights of the rushing train
dispel the dawn's doom

Leaky byre at dusk —
thin cows lean out their sad heads
towards bleak pastures

Brief Brooklyn blackouts —
chilly wind ruffles her hair
as she smiles at stars

Two cops break the law
to hide from the pounding rain
while thieves shake with cold

The drops of hot blood
dripping into the catch pit;
the clubbing goes on

The coughing orphan
in the cloud of noxious fumes;
late night on the streets

Drinking her latte
she looks at the blind fiddler
playing mournful tunes

The belching steam train
speeds past the unspoilt oak holt;
the shamefaced driver

The blind-drunk farmhand
forgets to bolt the croft's gate;
approaching deep growls

The drab's vacant eyes
deepen this evening's damp chill;
the unwarmed creep joint

Sweet repose for moths —
the glow of buzzing streetlamps
soaking in the rain

This mute orphan girl
locked in the old pervert's flat
will never be found

A lone, wounded wolf
barks wildly at the full moon
until his voice dies

On this night so dark
an injured rat climbs the path
to the misty hills

A pregnant cat springs
onto the clean mantelpiece;
brass vase falls and breaks

The birds are asleep —
a sudden hail of dry leaves
makes the sly fox shake

Autumnal windfall —
father's death in the orchard
in a raging storm

Her slender fingers
fondle my sun-kissed shoulders;
the delayed owl-light

Power plant at dusk —
a skein of cranes heading south
through pink clouds of smoke

When the brass bell blares
thin mist rolls over the fields;
hazy sun at dusk

Green downs at sundown —
a buzzard hangs motionless
in the windless air

Watching the blue sky
a huge spider knits the web
to catch one small fly

The clock strikes the hour —
the matron's colourless face
in the cool crow-time

Secluded hedge maze —
an old rook's sorrowful song
in the evening rain

Savage stray dogs race
through the empty train station;
trains dare not come here

On black, slick rooftops —
as the thief crawls up the ridge
his legs slide backwards

Twinkling gemmed sceptre
on the baron's soft cushion;
dark shadow creeps past

Unnamed country road —
drunk josser falls to the ditch
where tall nettles grow

Lunatic harness —
confined within moonlit yard
oxen roar fiercely

Approaching menace —
boys fall down the secret stair
onto the cow dung

Delicate fragrance
of smooth and creamy coffee
fills her room with warmth

The toss of a coin —
fear grips these starlit bandits
as they lose their wits

Crossing the green lane
an elk brings some yellow leaves
on his bog-moist hooves

Cold rain starts to fall
as she unbuttons my coat;
farewell at the pier

The reek of petrol —
baby boomer's mangled legs
on his well-trimmed lawn

Rain and smooth cello
make these harsh techno soundscapes
sweet-tuned to young wrens

Approaching sirens —
he turns off the radio
and lets her child sleep

On this stormy night
guns are blazing in the mall;
Black Friday goes *right*

Pumpkin spice latte
spilled on her voguish sweater;
green mermaid chuckles

Two lively brimstones
flitting around sleepy hares
that bask in the sun

A small penny bun
amid the hosts of death caps
swarming with black flies

Sunlit chanterelles
in the forsaken basket
laid on the soft moss

The rooster's shrill call
echoes in the brisk dawn air;
the tang of mowed hay

Distant cries of gulls
fade out with the ruddy sun
setting in the west

When the mizzle stops
shafts of watery sunlight
fill the misty glen

A wounded falcon
perches on the tall maple;
gold and blood mingle

Early dawn chorus —
a tabby cat stalking birds
in the golden mist

This one-eyed stray cat
has never seen any birds
from his cellar jail

This chained, frail mongrel
has never left his small yard
and will die there too

An empty kennel —
chains clank in the midnight air
on this remote farm

False dawn at the slum —
two stray cats hiss angrily
at these sleeping tramps

Moonless back alley —
sardines in a crushed tin box
lure twelve hungry cats

In this moon-shaped pool
daydreaming eyes are so blurred;
rainy witching hour

A strong tide comes in —
a gang of drunken beach bums
sleeping on the dunes

On these lamplit hills
the thugs find no dark shadows
to wait in ambush

Late afternoon (f)light —
the boy eats cauliflower
above puffy clouds

The shepherd's shrewd eye
catches the sight of his sheep
strayed in the thick fog

Empty streets at night —
when the pelting rain lifts up
the air becomes fresh

Murky cock-shut light —
rain drones on the leaky roof
of this quaint chapel

Undone button flies —
when he unlocks the outhouse
swarms of flies pour out

Night before logging —
a lynx glares at the full moon
eclipsed by tall firs

The breathless jogger
reaches his warm home just as
the flood tide sweeps in

Frigid storm-force wind
whips up dust in the quarry;
time for a lunch break

A thick-bodied snake
slithers across the wet road;
screeching of the tyres

It's oh so quiet —
the smell of burning dead leaves
fills the breezeless air

A forlorn graveyard —
the crow's dolorous cawing
through the faint drizzle

His failed catcalling —
two stray cats look back in fear
while she ignores him

In the pouring rain
a small snail creeps on snail mail
not opened today

A young girl's flushed cheeks
as she enters the kitchen;
apples in her trug

The widow's last stroll —
cold air slides down the hillside
as September fleets

Farewell to summer —
as we stand on the dark bridge
her life flows away

Drowning in deep ditch
these drunk diggers dig despite
the driving downpour

The low of a calf
left in the driving rainstorm
that haunts this bare plain

Their twelfth jubilee —
sweet fragrance of apple pie
fills the quaint cottage

The garth's twilight hour —
distant traffic murmuring
through wall wrapped in vine

Bums dressed in smart suits
sip mulled wine from thieved glasses;
mansion heist goes wrong

Evening petrichor —
the fresh breeze stirs her French braids
as she drinks green tea

Gauzy gossamers
float onto a floral frock
hanging on the string

A bar of chocolate
hidden deep in the cupboard;
my grandma's solace

Filigree swallows
sit unstirred on power lines;
fields in flames and gold

Morning birdwatching —
the boy slips across the streets
on swift, silent feet

A gnarled apple tree
bends towards the roofless barn;
high wind sheds its leaves

The child's final jump —
sharp rock hidden under leaves
tears his head apart

Fog on the barrows —
rabbits shiver in the chill
that dews their burrow

Wrapped in a thick coat
she stares at the falling leaves
burying her alive

A repulsive musk —
a hungry weasel ignores
the shrew's dead body

Doors squeal in the squall —
a derelict hunting lodge
filled with marten's scats

Squeaks in the dark spire;
a lone rat loses its tooth
as the owl swoops down

An eyeless foundling
chained to the earless vagrant;
mute screams in the crypt

Approaching footsteps
on the spiralling staircase
dappled in starlight

The priest's lone vigil —
candles brighten the coffin
in this murky crypt

FURTHER READING

The following section contains a list of works which the reader may consult for additional information and context about the religious or historical traditions depicted in the poems.

L. Alcock – *Arthur's Britain*
M. Aldhouse-Green – *Animals in Celtic Life and Myth*
M. Aldhouse-Green – *The Celtic World*
M. Aldhouse-Green – *Dictionary of Celtic Myth and Legend*
E. Bhreathnach – *Ireland in the Medieval World AD 400-100*
A. Carmichael – *Carmina Gadelica*
A. Carmichael – *Popular Tales of the West Highlands*
J. Caesar – *The Gallic War*
N. Chadwick – *The Celtic Realms*
T. Clarkson – *The Men of the North*
B. Cunliffe – *The Ancient Celts*
B. Cunliffe – *Iron Age Communities in Britain*
P. Ellis – *The Druids*
P. V. Glob – *The Bog People: Iron-Age Man Preserved*
I. A. Gregory – *Gods and Fighting Men*
I. A. Gregory – *Visions and Beliefs in the West of Ireland*
J. Halliwell-Phillipps – *A Dictionary of Archaic and Provincial Words*
P. W. Joyce – *A Smaller Social History of Ancient Ireland*
A. Moffat – *Arthur and the Lost Kingdoms*
A. Moffat – *The Faded Map: Lost Kingdoms of Scotland*
A. Moffat – *To the Island of Tides: A Journey to Lindisfarne*
J. Morris – *The Age of Arthur*
P. Monaghan – *The Encyclopedia of Celtic Myth and Folklore*
J. Koch – *Celtic Culture. A Historical Encyclopedia*
A. Konstam – *Strongholds of the Picts*
D. Ó Cróinín – *Early Medieval Ireland 400-1200*
T. F. O'Rahilly – *Early Irish History and Mythology*
C. A. Snyder – *An Age of Tyrants*
C. Tacitus – *Agricola*
M. Trevelyan – *Folk-lore and Folk-stories of Wales*
W. J. Watson – *The Celtic Place-names of Scotland*